T0086238

The Golden Thread

Making Healthcare Decisions
in Neighborhoods

M. Margaret McDonnell, RSCJ

BALBOA.PRESS
A DIVISION OF HAY HOUSE

Balboa Press books may be ordered through booksellers or by contacting:

Balboa Press
A Division of Hay House
1663 Liberty Drive
Bloomington, IN 47403
www.balboapress.com
844-682-1282

Because of the dynamic nature of the Internet, any web addresses or
links contained in this book may have changed since publication and
may no longer be valid. The views expressed in this work are solely those
of the author and do not necessarily reflect the views of the publisher,
and the publisher hereby disclaims any responsibility for them.

The author of this book does not dispense medical advice or prescribe the use
of any technique as a form of treatment for physical, emotional, or medical
problems without the advice of a physician, either directly or indirectly. The
intent of the author is only to offer information of a general nature to help
you in your quest for emotional and spiritual well-being. In the event you use
any of the information in this book for yourself, which is your constitutional
right, the author and the publisher assume no responsibility for your actions.

Any people depicted in stock imagery provided by Getty Images are
models, and such images are being used for illustrative purposes only.
Certain stock imagery © Getty Images.

Print information available on the last page.

ISBN: 978-1-9822-7874-8 (sc)
ISBN: 978-1-9822-7875-5 (e)

Balboa Press rev. date: 02/09/2022

DEDICATION

In Memory of Janet Barber

CONTENTS

ACKNOWLEDGEMENTS

The Interns at The Center for Ethics and Advocacy in Healthcare

Christine DeLuca 1998
Timothy O'Rourke 1999-2001
Christopher Grodecki, SJ 2000
James Buino, JD 2001
Sarah Matos 2002
James Shay, JD 2002
Lann Choi 2003
Rachel Jennings, JD 2003-2004
Gabriella Lazcano 2003
Borim Yang 2003
Lauren Harlow 2004
Zach Sufrin 2004
Rick Gaines, MD
Michelle Lerman 2005
Jacob Levin 2004
Erin O'Donnell-Dotzler 2005
Sarah Colten 2006
Richard Nelson 2006
Ashanti Riles 2006
Anna Bittman 2007
Gabriella Sacco 2007
Alex Valvassori 2007
Madalyn Guy 2008
Jingpin Li 2008
Andrea Tamillo 2008
Jason Altilio, PhD.2009-2012

Anam Aslam, MD 2009
Katie Duncan 2009
Lani Leong 2009
Katie Special 2009-2011
Tanuka Raj 2010
Roshea Williams 2010
Clare Whylie 2010
Nirali Dave 2011
Prihy Mehta 2011
Nikiti Saladi 2011
Kathleen Wallace, JD 2011
Emily Breitbart 2012
Anne Carroll 2012
Kahlia Keita 2012
Cynthia Russo 2012
Dennis Trimboli, JD
Molly Chale 2013

In addition to the students, without whom this work
would never have been possible, I acknowledge
with deep appreciation the following people:
Robert Brill, editor
The sick who have taught me
The many who have been readers as this
book was made ready for publishing

TESTIMONIALS

Sister Peggy McDonnell told me in an interview a few years ago that she would go to the "ends of the earth" for a sick person. That phrase encapsulates her total dedication to her work as a nun, nurse, and medical ethicist. In *The Golden Thread*, Sister Peggy says that a patient must become a critical part of the decision-making process that determines the final passage of life. Indeed, robbing a dying person of this crucial role, she says, makes the possibility of growing into full personhood—even at the end of life—much harder. It is that kind of practical wisdom about ethics that makes *The Golden Thread* such a vital book on the topic of end-of-life care. Inside its pages, there is a wealth of insight into the life work of Sister Peggy, and its overall message invites us to use her tried-and-true practices in our own communities.

Holly Marihugh, M.A., Writer and Speaker

The Golden Thread by Sister Peggy McDonnell is an aptly titled book weaving practical patient advocacy together with the values of human dignity, respect, and the importance of personhood. As an early pioneer in the area of patient advocacy, she shares a decades-long journey of her work in the clinic, at the bedside, and as the founder of The Center for Ethics and Advocacy in Health Care. With a backdrop of genuine concern for community health and health care, McDonnell provides a practical decision-making framework for patients, families, and ethics committees dealing with ethical issues in patient care. Multiple real-world case studies provide helpful context. My own teaching and patient advocacy efforts have benefitted greatly from her experience and wisdom.

Tim Morris, Professor of Philosophy
Emeritus, North Central College

INTRODUCTION

In the fall of 1989 the ethics committee of a particular hospital began work on the issue of scarce resources. The process we embarked upon resulted in a method that will help to identify and evaluate similar cases, all having to do with outliers. More importantly, the work made us aware of the implications of patients' involvement in their own care. Thus, the project became a two-pronged one: identifying outliers and dealing with the ethical issues that lay behind the expenditures. Perhaps the most important of these issues turned out to be the capacity for knowing the reality of moral agency and participatory decision making on the part of the patient.

Methodology

From the start of this project, we used case studies followed by reflection on the ethical issues imbedded in each case. Meeting after meeting over one and one half years we would try to "get at" issues surrounding over expenditure. It became clear that we were in the middle of a process - method of learning to "do ethics".

At that time I reflected: In using this technique with a committee:

1. How does this, as opposed to a lecture method, affect the outcome of a discussion?
2. How does this method affect the ethical sensitivity of the group?
3. Does the group gain confidence in dealing with ethical decision-making?

It appeared that ethical sensitivity and a sense of security in dealing with moral dilemmas was greatly enhanced by using a process method. The group needed to be encouraged to continue to grapple with the issues as they unfolded. It was important to periodically summarize where the process was going. What was coming into view? It was important to have an educational session on the theory behind the ethical dilemma. In this case, the educational session was done on Moral Agency.

Assisting people on ethics committees to surface and name ethical issues is sometimes easy, sometimes difficult, depending on the material. What are the conflicting moral claims? What is or is not of moral significance? In some situations, a group may find it impossible to name all of the issues because of relationships around the table. The discussion of this case went on for some time since it was our intent to pursue some of the underlying issues to a greater extent than we ordinarily would, in hopes that we could get a "handle" on the resource issue.

Several things were marked throughout the process: First, there were efforts not to let any area of research go unaddressed. Second, there was a constant concern on the part of everyone that finances not become the overriding issue. Our ultimate concern was the patient. Our goal was to uncover the ethical issues imbedded behind the care being given.

The crux of the matter: It became clear in case after case that nothing was in place to safeguard participatory decision making for the sake of the patient. The challenge to the committee increasingly became: is there any way to "manage" practice patterns to the end that the patient would be involved in their own decision process? Is it not possible to have a provider chose specific behavior patterns towards the end that the patient will be his/her own moral agent? The experience of feeling that one has some control over one's destiny is energizing, life giving, at a time when the life of a patient could be threatened. This is patient autonomy. This is moral agency.

It became apparent as the work continued that, when the patient was not involved in his or her own decision process about care, ethical issues soared. We learned that practice patterns that were inconsistent with allowing the patient "full range of motion" in their care resulted in compromised care, with inability of the patient to be a participant in their own care.

The model we developed for inpatient situations quickly transitioned into the doing of community health care ethics, thus gathering members of families and extended communities around the person they loved as major life decisions were made.

In *The Golden Thread* I hope to make this kind of reflection of process understandable and therefore possible in order that small communities of people can gather around the sick and dying in their own neighborhood and town, thus enabling "base communities" to emerge not only in other countries around the world, but in our country as well. A Not for Profit arose out of this model in the late 1980's and the pages which follow tell the amazing story of what neighbors can come to mean to each other in times of illness and dying.

As this book was being written the world-wide Corona Virus Pandemic began. Health care resources were scarce both nation-wide and worldwide. It is my hope that this book, published as the pandemic is beginning to slow down, will offer us additional ways to reflect on the monumental health crisis that has impacted every one of us. Not only has it impacted us, patients and possible patients, but it has had a huge impact on the health care providers who have lived through days and months of caregiving under conditions of scarcity heretofore unheard of.

Imagine what it felt like to know that patients that were cared for and about might not live due to insufficient medical resources. Not enough oxygen, insufficient ventilators and more could be the reality of the situations. Perhaps as providers of care contracted Covid because of insufficient personal protective equipment people could begin to understand that these not-to-be-believed tragedies are happening here and now in our own country. We cannot fail to reflect on this terrible tragedy that has impacted our co-journeyers as this book is being written.

In summary, this book is about care-giving, community, being and becoming more moral people, making ethical decisions. It is about a Golden Thread wending its way through every life. The Golden Thread becomes more important than anything else, but identifying and tracing this Golden Thread becomes not just a challenge but the thrill of each lifetime.

CHAPTER ONE

MAKING HEALTHCARE DECISIONS IN NEIGHBORHOODS

As a healthcare provider for many years, I have to say that my *passion* never wanes. Now in my eighties, I remain alive with passion for the sick. I had intended that this book be entitled *A Community Healthcare Ethics Teaching Manual* but have been told by a number of people that it is really a memoir because it is in chronological order.

I have also been told that the story is remarkable. I know why. The hand of God has guided me every step of the way and now as I reflect on my life's work, I realize that this passion emerged as I wrote what, in a clinical setting, would be chart notes about sick patients for whom I cared. I simply did what I loved to do, and I wrote what seemed apparent to me. However, in reading these stories in later years, the way I have expressed the reality of each patient tells me that there has been a Golden Thread weaving its way through the life of each patient. I call this reality God. I would never have known that I was being so guided as I laid my hands on in caregiving. As I reflect on it all now, I am certain.

When I was at Boston's North End Community Health Center in the late 1970s, growing increasingly weary after many years working as a healthcare practitioner, I struggled with the question: What can I do to bring spirituality into healthcare? At that time, one could not make a profession of bringing spirituality into healthcare. There was pastoral care, but as I considered getting a degree in that field, I realized it was not really hitting the mark when it came to problems I wanted to address in my day-to-day practice. As I thought about my clinical experience and exactly what it was that I wanted to go deeply into, I could not name a professional degree that went to the depths of my personal interior experience. One day Father James O'Donohue, a colleague and an archdiocesan priest in Boston, said to me, "Peggy, you belong in ethics." Jim had known me for a long time, so he was able to understand very deeply the struggle in which I was engaged. Jim was a moral theologian and a medical ethicist, practicing in that capacity in the Boston area. That seemed impossible, but I assented with a nod of my head and went off to dwell in this idea.

Fast forward to the academic year of 1979-1980, and I was applying to the Harvard Divinity School for a degree in healthcare ethics. I was accepted into the program. The environment was exhilarating. Many healthcare practitioners were there that fall, and all of us were struggling with questions of ethics. After class on Mondays, I went by MTA to Chelsea where, in the evening, I staffed the neighborhood health center.

My inner world became as enriched with the philosophical issues of Justice and Love as it was with the spiritual issues of Justice and Love. In retrospect, Justice and Love gradually morphed into spiritual/philosophical concepts, and I slowly began to live with the merged reality and my changing mode of discernment in a completely new way. I could encounter an ethical issue and fully understand it in its spiritual dimensions after silence and reflection.

From the 1980s until 2016, my work involved visiting the sick in small local communities and going into homes. From 1995 to 2016, I worked from a freestanding not for profit, The Center for Ethics and Advocacy in Healthcare. I saw the Golden

Thread woven through encounters with wonderful people. My desire to teach others how to make difficult healthcare decisions, particularly at the end of life and outside of a hospital setting, definitely powered me to enter more deeply into the lives of vulnerable people. Their open wounds, psychologically speaking, were so welcoming. Their physical wounds called for answers to questions and invited their stories.

As a child, the seeds of the main work of my life were already planted. I did not know this until my later years. Diagnosed with a chronic systemic illness in my early thirties, I could not help but reflect on the many patients who had encouraged me. My innate passion for sick people had always been undergirded by God. I gradually became more conscious of this.

The combination of physical or mental vulnerability in patients who have to make extremely difficult decisions when critically ill allowed the power of God to show through and be manifested in the sick person. The sight was overpowering to me. The sick people might have felt themselves unable to communicate with anyone, let alone God, but God "overtook" to the point that I, a relative bystander, was struck by what I saw. Little did I know that my future life's work would unfold during these younger years. I would leave patients' homes, go to my car and tape what I heard or saw into a small tape recorder. Later a wonderful volunteer typed these case studies, and I held these treasures in my own "vessel of clay," my Self.

Some of the stories are included in this book. Many of the educational materials used by those of us working in the field of healthcare ethics during the 1980s, 1990s, and around the turn of the century are also included. The process of discerning *correct* healthcare decisions factored into how each patient brought closure to his or her life. Thus, the power of choice and assisting patients through their evolution into full personhood as death approached

3

became profoundly important. People at such junctures in life have many decisions to make, and the circumstances under which these are made can be so difficult. Additionally, the materials used by healthcare providers to aid in decision-making were not easily understood. In the 1980s, when this was all so new, technological advances made such decisions much more complex. Those of us doing healthcare ethics created materials specifically for complex situations. Members of ethics committees were helping to drive "patient self-determination." My work with ethics committees in the 1980s helped me hone the original materials, and in the 1990s I began to adapt them for use in the neighborhood and in homes. In healthcare facilities, the Patient Self-Determination Act affected admission procedures. This actually necessitated the starting of ethics committees because the new law required "information to be given to adult patients about their rights under state laws governing advance directives, including: 1) the right to participate in and direct their own healthcare decisions; 2) the right to accept or refuse medical or surgical treatment; 3) the right to prepare an advance directive."[1]

The Golden Thread is the name I personally gave to this manifestation of God within sick individuals as their personhood developed during serious illness. I saw what patients themselves could not see during times of suffering. I reflected this back to them, and they began to believe in their struggle to live, perhaps as they lay dying.

I observed that patients at the end of their lives frequently began to focus on a far-off Point. That Point led them on. I capitalize "Point" because I believe God is the Point. I see their gaze focus, sharpen. They start to move toward it, or perhaps better said, their eyes follow the Point. It becomes harder and harder for me to take their attention from the Point when I speak to them. I never want to nor would I break into their profound silence.

As these patients experience increasingly compromised health, they also begin to refine their choices to follow the Point. Their decisions at such a time reveal their choice for this Point. I now am certain that this choice is for this deep unseen source of their Higher Power. Each person calls their Higher Power by a different name. For me, it is God. Again, all of this explains the Golden Thread. Pain can be both physical and psychological. It is frequently present. As time and the disease process continue, these can interfere with and disturb what family members looking on might hope would be a peaceful time. However, the deep interior process that I describe in a patient is not broken.

In reading the narratives of those who are seriously ill, although perhaps not noticeably in danger of death, I realize that their awareness of a deeper Higher Power within them can be manifested differently. This is not a qualitative "better" or "worse" situation.

For critically ill and dying people, one disturbing force can be the cost of their care. Patients are often aware of this. Tensions increase around a bed for many reasons. In such instances, I frequently observed that patients were less able to be involved in their own decision-making, and end-of-life decisions were much harder to make for both patients and their family. For example, an aging couple may disagree on the correct course of care, the dying wife wanting less treatment, and the husband perhaps insisting on continuing aggressive treatment. Physician and nurse "practice patterns" might be inconsistent with allowing the sick or dying persons "full range of motion" in their care, thus stunting, or compromising inner growth. (Practice patterns are medical and nursing practices associated with a particular aspect of care.) Patients can be very perceptive when they are seriously ill and not miss a thing.

For an onlooker who may hold multiple non-caregiving responsibilities, it becomes harder to notice the dynamics of a relationship with the patients' Higher Power. The stress of these moments interferes with the insight of the onlookers, who may be so dazed by all that is happening that they are rendered incapable of noticing these profound moments.

If patients are not full participants in decisions made, the concerns of others can create pressure. The speed of life in a hospital setting can also make such times stressful for patients. Such circumstances breaking into their silence prevent them from being fully themselves. On the other hand, others can subtly become the decision makers.

In summary, patients must make their own decisions or at least be decision participants unless they are medically or psychologically incapable. Pressure in any form is unethical.

Having been taught by patients, I believe in their struggles and in this memoir, I explain what I have seen. Patient narratives, a literary genre that has emerged in recent years, indicate that when patients are allowed the opportunity to express their journey with trusted family and friends, they can refine their choices. They become increasingly certain of this unfolding story. Their choices continue to clarify the "why" of their existence; their lives begin to make sense to them even though they are very vulnerable. If they are not able to be decision participants, they can often unintentionally assume a "dependent interior posture." They start to lean on others to make the decisions. This makes the possibility of growing to full personhood much harder, and interior suffering is made worse.

This book is intended for families, individuals and communities. A wisdom community refers to those who are closest to any person in a family and is the group that knows them best. The knowledge base of this group of people is such that the word wisdom speaks of the depth of knowledge that they together hold about a person. I hope that these pages might serve as a thoughtful companion on the journey that shapes our lives into whatever our future may be.

My hope is also that the stories that I have included teach us that growth into full personhood is possible during such struggles with health. This is true as people are assisted in the process of making decisions along with nurses, doctors and other providers of care. Ethical dilemmas or conflicts in values often are embedded in the stories. The values of each player in a story are made clear as conflicts about decisions are resolved, as decisions are made. I have included in the text and the appendix educational materials that can teach us how to make such decisions.

In the 1980s, hospital and nursing home ethics committee members were learning to "do ethics." At the same time, they were also becoming increasingly sensitive as they watched people change during illness and dying. The method for resolving decisions could be modified as ethics committee members learned and gained experience, thus again putting personhood first as decisions were made. Increasingly, the concept of personhood came to be appreciated.

At the core of vulnerability is loss of dignity. People are forced to change or let go of cherished assumptions and values. They must recreate their life story in order to regain their identity. Their personhood is at stake though they may not think of using this word. They need to rediscover and rename their boundaries (as in "I can go no further") and restore their sense of inner security.

The task of each one of us when helping sick persons is to assist them in reorganizing their life story so that it can make sense in their new inner and perhaps outer environment. During such a process a patient, who is above all a person, comes to a new understanding of Self and is empowered to reformulate the organizing story of his or her life. All of this actually forms a new identity for the person, or, as the ethicist Warren Reich expresses it in his book, *Models of Pain and Suffering*, a "regained autonomy."[2]

So the shift from a dependent role and the taking on of a position of patient autonomy, not to mention the incoming of Love so subtly in the life of a critically ill patient, transforms the person and makes him or her ready for life to continue or for the moment of death. This transformation takes place in what is called their Centerspace. Our Centerspace is the spiritual-psychological "location" of the coalescence of our thinking, feelings and value system. This evolution of personhood during illness, if writing, is called in today's literature, an illness narrative.

People on ethics committees thus become participants in the great story of human growth. Sick people are honored as their life stories become known. The challenge to ethics committees is to advise healthcare practitioners, patients and families in such a way that values can be clarified and more deeply appreciated. Patients must, insofar as possible, have control over their destiny. This encourages patient autonomy. It allows patients the power to "choose life" even as they may be dying because the patient can exercise the power of choice. Choosing life becomes choosing Life (with a capital L) as the Golden Thread becomes a deeper, Higher Power within. Having a choice is life giving. It is empowering. It provides people with self-confidence.

During the 1990s, in my capacity as a community healthcare ethicist, I became aware that people frequently made serious decisions while at home and not in a hospital. Times were changing. I went into their homes at their request, or perhaps offered advice as requested when I encountered people I knew on the street. Longtime residents who had come to know and trust me would call or come to the place where I lived in the same community, or I would go to their workplace. I followed up with people after an initial "encounter" (the name frequently used for a patient-physician appointment after the 1990s) to be sure things were on track. They would not necessarily need an ethicist, but word traveled about my background. They felt confident that, if I knew their thinking, I would affirm or not the decision they had reached or were considering. The time had come for families of patients and patients themselves to know how to make these decisions because of the lack of structures in neighborhoods and communities to assist in healthcare decision-making.

When those whom I knew were sick, I would often think about them as I awoke in the morning and call them as soon as possible to see how they were doing. Very occasionally, I received calls during the night, and I would go to homes in an emergency. Patients felt as though a call to a doctor might result in an appointment some days or weeks away, when to them the need was more urgent. If they felt this way, they would, as far back as the 1990s, stop at my door or call me, perhaps indicative of their need to simply ease a concern.

This emerging culture nationwide typified what slowly came to be known as de-institutionalized healthcare. As a result, people had more questions about their care and about upcoming procedures while in neighborhoods, and perhaps they were apprehensive. Had they made the right decisions? Because of working in neighborhoods in my own community, I was, in a way, freed from institutional structural constraints. People knew that. In a sense, we were all freer. They never abused my availability, and I, in turn, could always be honest if I felt I could not answer accurately, be immediately available, or wanted to consult someone else. Often my advice would be to see their local physician as quickly as possible.

Community healthcare emerged gradually as various community services (home care, laboratory test services, physical therapy, for example) emerged. Other healthcare professionals often lived in these neighborhoods and they would be readily available to help a neighbor. I developed a model for a community-based ethics consultation center (in 1996 The Center for Ethics and Advocacy in Healthcare officially became an Illinois not for profit.) With a healthcare ethics background and as a nurse practitioner in community health, I transitioned into doing community-based healthcare ethics full time. At the same time, hospital ethics committees were completing their education, and there was less need for consultants. In neighborhoods, families gathered around the dining room table to discuss life and death decisions. People were dealing with so much in neighborhoods. In emergencies, simply calling an ambulance could be an emotionally hard decision for a family suffering financially. On one occasion, I was called to a home very early one morning and arrived quickly, though after the ambulance left. Understandably, the family was terribly upset. The husband and father had died suddenly.

The Golden Thread was also weaving a path through me in these times. I realize now that it was the presence of God within me as I lived through each day, and it had a very unusual pattern. This was not an idea I had; it was an inspiration. This was God working in and through me. Now as I tell the story, it is the story of those who inspired me as well as my own story. My passion deepened as we taught one another. A Healing Community began.

---

[1] Patient Self Determination Act of 1990 (H.R. 4449): https://www.congress.gov/bill/101st-congress/house-bill/ 4449.

[2] Reich, Warren Thomas, "Models of Pain and Suffering: Foundations for an Ethic of Compassion" (Conference Paper), part of *Acta Neurochirurgica Supplementum*, Volume 38, 1987, Springer-Verlag, New York.

CHAPTER TWO

BECOMING WHO WE ARE

EXPERIENCES AS A CHILD PROBABLY FORMED ME MORE THAN I realize. As a 13-year-old, I began volunteering as a candy striper in our local hospital, Riverview, in Red Bank, New Jersey. I was placed in the ob-gyn unit and saw deliveries, helped post-partum women as a very young woman who was between seventh and eighth grades. A fine nurse named Helen Riegelman mentored me. I often remember her as being so wise, personally gifted, and compassionate. In recent months, I found her family on Facebook. When I posted a message in search of her, seven to ten women, including one of her nieces, responded. Everyone expressed the same thing: Miss Riegelman had changed their lives too. I was astounded.

I was deeply impressed by the fact that patients were not in charge of their lives in those years, 1953 and 1954. Doctors were.[3] I saw things I cannot speak about here, but I saw, I understood, and I said nothing. In photos of me as a child, I notice myself as one who held a lot within. I was silent. I held a secret. I was being formed in a profound way: We have the right to choose. We hold a responsibility far more profound than we can imagine.

The Jesuit theologian George Aschenbrunner, SJ, said, "The issue of control is the most important because it involves our power to decide. That is a power that even God does not interfere with, since it is the difference between being a person and a puppet. God chooses to create human beings as persons. So, the gift of the power of choice is characteristic both of God and of the persons that God chooses to create."[4]

I noticed that sick people often had the power of choice taken from them. Here I was becoming a woman for whom the power of choice was clearly pivotal. I did not have any idea that this was happening to me. I recall many huge decisions I had to make as a nurse. I would frequently stand in place and ask myself: What should I do? Times of illness involve difficult journeys, and my hope is that these pages might serve as a thoughtful companion on our journey as we shape our lives into whatever future is planned for us.

As a young student nurse in the late 1950s, I had three pivotal experiences that shaped my life for the remainder of my years. Now 83, although I can no longer do hands-on care, I remain truly passionate about sick people. I simply love people; sick people draw me; the sicker people are, the more they draw me. Love is called forth from me. Sick people are irresistible. My passion has grown deeper as the years have passed. This passion has driven me to develop the main work of my life: advocating for the sick no matter their income level, and helping people make ethical decisions about their life choices during illness, so they can live while dying. I do not even need to be near them to feel this "draw." My depth of feeling goes far beneath. I do not even need to be at the bedside. This draw literally draws me.

The first pivotal experience occurred when I was caring for a man with a very large, abdominal wound. The surgery was some days past and the stitches broke, leaving a gaping abdominal wound. I was responsible for his care that day and getting him ready for a second operation. I remember being so afraid for this man. I wanted to do everything perfectly so that he would "make it." Being this scared I forgot to take his socks off, and as I wheeled him into the elevator to go to the OR, his feet were the last to go in and I saw those socks. I have no memory of what I did then. I hope I took them off. Indelibly imprinted in my memory is one image that has stayed with me throughout my life: The open wound, *not* the socks! The image of that wound has fortified me repeatedly as I have talked to people in pain and those who are dying. It has fortified me during my own moments of physical, emotional, and spiritual pain. We students cared for that man after he returned to his room — day in and day out. We packed new gauze into the wound four times a day, allowing it to heal from the inside out. The surgeons feared that if they sutured it again, it would break open. Best to let it heal from the inside out. It took a long time.

Wounds do heal from the inside out. The abdomen is large and the tissue there runs deep. Filling this wound-space and forming a scar is a process that requires time and patience—and a caregiver's constant watching. The scar, once formed, is then secure and cannot be compromised. The deeper the scar, the safer the abdominal wall will be. Likewise, the deeper the wound from any inner pain, the more inner growth there will be. Creativity arises from such psychological scars if we allow it. This experience has given me more patience with my own healing processes, and I am in a position to teach others the same thing time and time again.

The second experience was on a surgical ward with about a dozen patients. I had worked the night shift. It was approaching 7 a.m. The priest was about to bring communion to our floor, a daily ritual. Every morning at that time, everyone receiving communion had to be "ready." I gave each person a washcloth and toothbrush and straightened their beds. Not much more at this moment. I was responsible for giving out morning medications, including, on that day, pre-op meds. There were three wards on this surgical floor. In my haste, while in one ward, I switched the injections for two women, giving one the contents of the syringe in my right hand, and the woman next to her the injection in my left hand. I should have done the reverse. Little did I know that the journey of the rest of my life had begun. I stood in the middle of that ward for one horrifying moment realizing what I had done, facing myself, knowing it happened because I was hurrying and I was so tired after the night shift. What would happen if I told the supervisor? Would the two women be all right? Could they die because of what I did? I also asked myself: How can I best live with this decision?

This was *the* ethical moment of my life; it was "the first day of the rest of my life." I told the supervisor, and I was suspended. It was a very light "sentence" for what I had done, but I was devastated. I was sure my life was ruined. I did not then realize how passionate I was about doing caregiving in the right way for suffering people, but also about being honest, first of all, with myself. I was passionate about doing the right thing. I thought my career in nursing was ruined. "I was finished," as they say. Most importantly: Could someone die because of what I did? My developing passion has been wiped out, or so I thought.

When I got off duty that morning, having told the supervisor, I went to a pay phone. I was afraid that if I called my parents from the corridor phone in the nurses' residence, someone might overhear me, so I went to the phone across from the hospital. I thought I could never tell my classmates what had happened, but I told my mother. She said: "Of course, we will take you home!" So home I went for two weeks.

A third pivotal experience was this: We student nurses were told that if we were out in public, or outside of the hospital setting, we should never run to rescue someone or get involved in an accident scene. We could be held liable. One day I was out for a walk near the hospital when an elderly man fell right in the middle of a busy intersection. I ran to help him get up so he would not be hit by oncoming traffic. Someone else came to help and we got him to the sidewalk. He was not seriously injured. This passion of mine would never have allowed me to stand in place. Without a thought, any one of us would have done what I did. This kind of rigorous work is passion-driven. The rigor of the schedule, the relentless suffering on the part of patients, the need for constant coordination of services in order to save lives, the constant need to refrain from emotional reactions to events and people's responses to them: a steadiness of spirit and a rootedness in one's Self are required.(The capital "S" implying God-in-us), that only people of passion could endure.

In the late 1970s, I was a nurse practitioner in a small neighborhood health center in Boston's North End. People from all economic brackets came in, either scheduled or as walk-ins. Day after day, I saw people who had very little in the way of financial resources. These were really sick people for the most part. Finally, I decided that I had to figure out how to survive in the healthcare system, having seen low-income people up against such great odds time and time again. I thought: "I have to find a way to stay in the system or I have to get out." I was in my late thirties. I wanted to stay in nursing so badly, but how could I survive if I wanted to continue to work with those with insufficient financial resources? How could I look them in the eye, know what they knew and live with it?

After several years of soul searching, I asked to go on for further studies in the field of healthcare ethics. That was when I was blessed to begin my studies at the Harvard Divinity School. Confronted with so many questions of ethics, I couldn't imagine that there would be any one answer that would help. I came to realize that each situation would need a separate answer. However, as I was about to graduate, I did find *the* question with which I could live the remainder of my life: How do Love and Justice intersect in a world of scarce medical resources? I also realized that *there was no answer to my struggle;* there would only be the same question coming back repeatedly. Perhaps even more importantly, I found the following words by Rainer Maria Rilke in *Letters to a Young Poet:*

> Be patient toward all that is unresolved in your heart and try to love the questions themselves, like locked rooms and like books that are now written in a very foreign tongue. Do not now seek the answers, which cannot be given you because you would not be able to live them. And the point is, to live everything. Live the questions now. Perhaps you will then gradually, without noticing it, live along some distant day into the answer.[5]

I knew I had found my question, and I continue to live my life in search of the answer. My passion and my question are with me still, and so I have begun "the first day of the rest of my life" in writing this book. I might add that the word character, according to Robert Coles, refers to how we behave when others are not looking. Little did I know how important this extraordinary and painful life experience would prove to be as I continued to try to live my life to the fullest.

---

[3] Gutman, Amy and Jonathon D. Moreno. *Everybody Wants To Go To Heaven But Nobody Wants to Die.* New York: Liveright Publishing Corporation, New York. 2019.

[4] Aschenbrunner, SJ. Unpublished Papers

[5] Rainer Maria Rilke, from *Letters to a Young Poet*, in *Selected Poems*, Methuen, New Jersey: 1986. p.12.

CHAPTER THREE

BEGINNINGS IN THE NEIGHBORHOOD

"Welcome! Hello, Peggy! Come in!" One time, a call came from a desperate father in Washington, D.C. He and his wife were trying to make a decision about their extremely ill child. I also received an email that brought me — though at a great distance — to the family of a woman faced with the decision to withdraw food and water from her terminally ill husband. All these events coalesced over many years to make it very clear that this effort was no small thing. I had a job. This was a ministry. I had a call. This was outpatient ethics, this was Community Healthcare Ethics.

The Center was not officially declared a not for profit until 1996, but to me it began in 1989. Specifically, that was when I moved from South Bend, Indiana, to the village of Winnetka, Illinois, just north of Chicago. There I rented a small apartment on the first floor of a two-flat building on Cherry Street. When leaving a position at the Holy Cross Health System in 1988, I had remained in South Bend to decide where in the country I should live. Having been born and raised on the North Jersey Shore, gone to schools in Philadelphia and New York, lived much of my religious life in Boston, I naturally leaned toward returning to my roots on the East Coast.

Since I was in my early fifties at this time, I still had a stretch of professional life ahead of me. I had no intention of starting a not for profit. Since the field of ethics in healthcare was still in its comparative infancy, I had to be sure that I was being professionally strategic in selecting my new place of residence. I had begun a consulting practice in ethics while still in South Bend and had one institutional client at the time of my move.

Some years later I was an ethics consultant in many Chicago-area hospitals. Then speaking engagements became part of my work-story. With a home office in Winnetka, I went out to hospitals and nursing homes from there. When I was home, I prepared for the ethics committee work. I started what I called an Inter-facility Ethics Committee in Long Term Care. Though I certainly knew that I was doing medical ethics, I did not stop to think beyond this. As I thought about it more, I read and learned that a new field had emerged known as applied medical ethics. It was offered as a major on many college campuses. I was doing just that: Applied Medical Ethics.

In my neighborhood, people mowed their own lawns and shoveled their own sidewalks. We had several block parties each year. This was a real community. We knew one another, our families, and our circumstances. Gradually trust grew. Word spread that I was a nurse by background and a nurse practitioner in community health. In addition, I was a Catholic nun, whatever that meant to people. I would be asked my views on certain topics, usually healthcare or religion, and discussion followed. A lot of mutual learning took place. We all learned that we could disagree at the level of value. Everyone was part of the conversation when such things came up.

People experiencing illness in the family came to my front door for help. Many times, a person in someone's extended family in another state became ill. One time a car pulled up and a neighbor of mine on the passenger side of the front seat rolled down her window. Her husband was driving and I went over to the car to talk to her. This was a very sick woman, though I would never have known it that day. Her arm and hand were affected. I soon learned it had been thought that she had carpel tunnel syndrome, but it turned out that she had terminal cancer. When she saw the doctor for her pre-op tests, Anne learned that in fact she had a brain tumor that had metastasized to her breast, with pain radiating to an arm and hand. I visited her at home during this illness. All of us on our block did. Anne died some months later. In retrospect, I think the car stopped that day because she needed to talk to me about dying. Not that she and I could have finished the topic that day, but it became the reason for my visits thereafter. I kept assuring her that I was "there." I am not sure that there were any difficult decisions to be made, but she and her husband both knew I was there for them.

Another day, I saw a car drive by and I recognized the driver as a nearby neighbor. Her small daughter was with her, and I saw her IV bag hanging from a hook over the backseat. My conversations thereafter were about the situation they were in, which started with the birth of their child with esophageal atresia, a narrowing of the esophagus. I got to know the family story and the social issues in the home. I was accepted into their environment no matter when or where we met. Conversation was easy. The child, now many years later, is a thriving young adult.

Another time I learned that Betty and her husband, who lived across the street, had had a terrible shock. Betty was found on the floor when her husband came home from work. She had had a slight stroke. Later, I realized that the ambulance passed me going in the other direction as I was on my way home the day it happened. I visited Betty in the hospital and she was doing quite well. She was there for two weeks. After returning home, she called me one day to tell me she was dying. I will never forget saying to her with a smile on my face: "Well, you don't sound like you are dying to me!" She laughed. I asked if I could come for tea. I did, and learned that Betty had been sent home with no support services, no physical therapy, no speech therapy, and no occupational therapy. She was alone all day. So, in fact, she felt as if she was dying. I started to visit several times a week, and Betty soon got well enough to get back to driving. Prior to this setback, she had worked as a sales clerk at a children's clothing shop in town. She was the "old style" sales person who helped customers try things on. She gave her opinion as to how the clothing looked and the like.

I don't think Betty was ever able to go back to work after her stroke, but she was able to stay busy and socialize. Then, during the first winter snowstorm of the year, while she was out doing an errand, Betty's car was broadsided at a bad intersection. I was the homilist at her funeral. It was a privilege to have been asked to do that. In the homily, I had written: "Last Sunday Betty called me and told me again, as she had in recent days, that she hadn't been feeling well. I said to her: "That's really scary isn't it"? She said: "That's why I called you." I went over to see her later that afternoon and asked her where her pain was. She made a gesture to her whole abdomen. Being a nurse, I laughed and said: "Not the whole thing! Point your finger to the place!" Betty laughed too. In the homily, I went on to say: "Since her stroke we all knew Betty had been less well. During these months and in recent weeks, Betty was beginning to realize, though perhaps unconsciously, that life was changing. God has been making her ready for this moment. This was the moment that God had chosen for her and Betty was ready. This might not have been our time, but it was Betty's time."

Then I quoted from a prayer by the French Jesuit philosopher and theologian Pierre Teilhard de Chardin. I said:

> Above all, trust in the slow work of God.
> We are quite naturally impatient in everything to

reach the end without delay.
We should like to skip the intermediate stages.
We are impatient of being on the way to something
unknown, something new.
And yet it is the law of all progress
that is made by passing through some stages of
instability—
and that may take a very long time.
And so I think it is with you;

Your ideas mature gradually. Let them grow.
Let them shape themselves without undue haste.
Do not try to force them on,
as though you could be today what time
(that is to say, grace and circumstances acting on
your own good will)
will make you tomorrow.
Only God could say what this new Spirit
gradually forming in you will be.
Give our Lord the benefit of believing
that His hand is leading you,
and accept the anxiety of feeling yourself
in suspense and incomplete.
Above all, trust in the slow work of God,
our loving vine-dresser.'"

My ethics consulting ministry evolved between 1990 and
1995 in Winnetka, at the intersection of Cherry and Provident
Streets. I would come and go, neighbors would come and go, and
suddenly a not for profit, The Center for Ethics and Advocacy
in Healthcare, was born. I hardly knew who I was becoming, or
whether that was part of the plan for my life as I had understood
it years ago. But there was a moment, more like a period of time,
when I said to myself, paraphrasing Martin Luther: "Here I am. I
can do no other." I asked permission of the Society of the Sacred

Heart to "put a frame around this ministry and make it a not for profit" because "this is the future of healthcare." I will forever be indebted to the very wise provincial who granted me permission.

In 1989, we Religious of the Sacred Heart had been asked by the Society of the Sacred Heart to embark on what we called a Social Analysis Project. Each of us was to state her ministry involvement at that time. I began: "I am a medical ethics consultant working with ethics committees in hospitals and nursing homes in Illinois; with individuals and families, teaching them how to make difficult treatment decisions; with administrators of hospitals (in dealing with the issue of scarce healthcare resources); with an Interfacility Ethics Committee in Long Term Care." Such committees had one member each from all represented facilities. In this way, each representative could benefit from hearing others' experience. The cost for each facility was only $50 per month for a one-hour session that would be benefit seven facilities. There was an urgency in getting this information out because it was all so new. There was another locus for my work. Because applied medical ethics was a new field and there were few with whom to network, we connected with other ethicists from various parts of the country to search for answers that could be obtained only through dialogue. Although I was consulting alone, I was not alone in my work.

The network of religious congregations in healthcare was well positioned to effect policy change because the congregations could afford to have well-developed ethics programs. I kept in constant contact with their directors of ethics in order to be united on issues around healthcare for the poor as well as other issues. The coordinating group for all of this was and remains the St. Louis-based Catholic Health Association. Its theology and ethics department serves as the hub for the ethics activities sponsored by religious congregations in healthcare.

My case-study approach was theoretical and practical. I assisted groups and individuals in identifying value priorities for their own lives and for institutions they administered. This resulted in moral growth at both institutional and personal levels.

Moral growth occurs when we deal with internal contradictions in our own moral reasoning structure, and when we come into conflict with the moral reasoning of others that is different from our own. In these situations, we oscillate from equilibrium to disequilibrium in our moral stance. How does one deal with individual values in a pluralistic world? While tension and conflict are productive of moral growth, how much tension can we sustain as we meet poles of paradoxes? I dealt with these questions in the healthcare setting.

The healthcare poor (frequently called the "underserved") are not necessarily grouped in economically deprived areas. They are people with inadequate health insurance (or none), as well as those who cannot take responsibility for their own decisions, resulting in their being left out of decisions made about their lives. They often both live and get healthcare outside of economically impoverished areas. After working for many years in neighborhood health centers among the poor and watching what was happening, I came to understand myself as being in an advocacy role for the underserved, a voice for the voiceless through the work of ethics committees. Continuing my response in the Social Analysis Project and moving on to the political factors, I identified the physician group as one of the factors. This was not to say that physicians were "the bad guys," nor was it by any means to say that the care they rendered was of poor quality. But I was saying that they were a strong group politically and they had an interest in not involving patients in their own care.

Physicians want people to live. Death is failure. Consequently, procedure after procedure may be done on the very frail. The cost of care is thus driven up, and patients lose the opportunity they must have to deal with the reality of sickness and death as consciously as possible. The face of physical diminishment is sometimes so alarming to physicians that they project onto patients a dependent role, or a "sick" role, which is a dependent one. This leads to the patient and family thinking that the physician is the only one who knows the way. This keeps the physician unchallenged about these patterns of practice, which all too frequently eliminate the patient from decision making and thus driving up the cost of care.

Addressing this in an ethics committee was a huge problem because to challenge this could risk losing the physician on the hospital staff and result in fewer admissions in a possibly already foundering hospital business. Many political problems stemmed from this central web, now institutionalized. A physician's patterns of care often evolved from this protective shell in which he or she had practiced for years.

Another important dimension of the political problem/ process was the hierarchical Church. Because I worked at that time in the circle of congregations whose work was healthcare, I was constantly keeping abreast of what the hierarchical Church was saying, trying to figure out how to keep communication open on certain issues while finding ways to stay on the side of the patient.

As to effecting change through the political process: I think the ethics movement is effecting "political" change. The problems are systemic, however; so it is taking time and it is often hard to see results. If I can help people to be sure about what they value and help them to be able to stand behind these values (when the going gets rough), then the patient can challenge the physician. But it is the unusual sick person who can be sick and challenge the very person upon whom life depends. The patients are the ones with the power. But because they are vulnerable, it is impossible for them to believe in their own power without someone advocating for them, someone who will in some cases stand right by them. Consumer ethics education has barely begun, but I see this movement to be extremely important. Many ethicists are moving into political advocacy, positioned well to effect systemic change. I see myself as one person in a network of people trying to help bring that about. Ethicists who take a stand on the many ethical issues gradually help to challenge the status quo involving economic, social and cultural factors.

There is a quest among people for a values base. It could rest in the history and traditions of communities. Perhaps it rests in and with the early faith communities and the communities of religious congregations, perhaps with the communities of moral philosophers who give verbal expression to lived morality in their times, or perhaps with a combination of these. Are we as a people returning to the traditions of these communities, returning to find resonance with their value systems? In finding resonance, we root and secure ourselves in traditions that speak to us of strength and stability. We rediscover ourselves. We are called forth at a time when we are unsure of our moral footing. We return and gather from the past what we need to move into the future. Any efforts made to set our sights on new horizons by returning to such value bases can contribute to a renewed human community.

In 1995, I moved to another apartment, also in Winnetka. The numbers of calls for actual assistance on my street noticeably increased. We stood out as a community that was coming together as illnesses of various kinds became evident. My move from Cherry Street necessitated separating the office from home. I established The Center for Ethics and Advocacy in Healthcare as an Illinois not for profit organization and received confirmation from the state in 1996. The office was located seven miles west of Winnetka on the grounds of the Conference Center of the Society of the Divine Word International in Techny, Illinois. The priests and brothers at Techny quietly became my brothers. They walked side by side with me for ten years until The Center closed in December 2015.

Our mission statement read: "The mission of The Center for Ethics and Advocacy in Healthcare is to educate individuals, families and institutions confronting the ethical implications of healthcare choices." It listed these four principles:

1. The Center recognizes the increasing complexity of healthcare decisions and believes that each individual is ultimately responsible for making healthcare decisions regarding his or her own life.
2. The Center recognizes that healthcare choices are affected by a number of inter-related factors and a circle of relationships.
3. The Center encourages a focused process in approaching healthcare decisions that involve consideration of the individual, the family, and healthcare providers.
4. The Center works to educate individuals, families, and institutions struggling with the ethical implications of healthcare decisions.

A 2008 documentary on The Center shows how the organization grew out of the emerging needs on Cherry Street in Winnetka. Initially I did not intend to start a Not for Profit. As I reflected on life on Cherry Street, I realized that, if we put a structure in place, it could do much good for people in the neighborhood.

Margaret Wheatley, who writes about leadership and organizational change, speaks to this reality in an article titled

"Reclaiming Gaia, Reclaiming Life": "Rather than thinking of organization as an imposed structure, plan, design, or role, it is clear that in life, organization arises from the interactions and needs of individuals who have decided to come together." She noted also: "Life seeks organization, but it uses messes to get there. Organization is a process, not a structure. ... If a new story has been given to you, it is time to tell it, wherever you are, to whomever you meet."[6]

With a belief in the new story that emerged both on Cherry Street and in myself, I spoke with my superior in the Society of the Sacred Heart about forming a not for profit. The healthcare incidents on Cherry Street impelled me to take a step forward in order to increase assistance for families in those neighborhoods where assistance was needed in making serious healthcare decisions at home. I recall asking my Provincial if we could "put a frame around what is happening," the frame being the Not for Profit structure. I received permission to proceed with setting up the Not for Profit. With both fear and hope in my heart, the new story emerged. I will be forever grateful to the leaders in the Society of the Sacred Heart.

People might comment: "But why in Winnetka, Illinois? These people appear to be financially well endowed." However, when the angel of death comes around the corner in any neighborhood, no one has adequate help. Everyone knows. Few people talk. Silence reigns. However, life is a journey. Life is a passage. People are rendered nonverbal because of fear. Everyone faces the need for help if a family member dies in a neighborhood. Death should not be faced alone unless one chooses to do so. The poet A.R. Ammons says in precise language in *Tape for the Turn of the Year*:

> Don't establish the
> boundaries
> first

the squares, triangles,
boxes,
of preconceived
possibility,
and then\pour
life into them, trimming
off left-over edges,
ending potential:
Let centers
proliferate
from
self-justifying motions!⁷

Therefore, we began. In 1993, four years after I moved to Winnetka, John ("Jack") Glaser, PhD, ethicist, and colleague, wrote, "The future will demand more than ever a community of likeminded, spiritually harmonious, and highly motivated members to continue the tradition of healthcare. This community will include religious and laypeople. It will be characterized by clarity of vision, commitment to a vision, sacrifice for a vision. The community of vision, commitment, and sacrifice needed to continue the healing mission of the churches goes beyond the present relationship of collaboration between religious congregations and laypersons who serve in governance and management capacities."

Jack went on to say that "social teaching emphasizes the central role of systems, structures, and institutions in accomplishing social justice." However, the new paradigm that he suggested was based primarily on passion for Gospel values. Other competencies follow far behind. "We must be prepared for new vehicles of grace. Once we begin to get specific about what justice means and demands we quickly realize that *there can be major differences between individuals' understandings of justice.*" (Italics mine.)

He concluded: "We need to create new structures of community affiliation and responsibility to carry on the healing ministry of the churches. Religious Congregations have a special responsibility and opportunity for leadership in creating this new community."[8]

Those involved in the effort begun on Cherry Street began to widen the existing web of community connections in order to serve those in very particular healthcare dilemmas. On my block, Liz had become terminally ill; Betty died three years after her stroke; Bill died very quietly at home; Maryanne cared for her young daughter at home; another neighbor, Anne, died of breast cancer. Will was born. All and more within the six years that I lived on Cherry Street.

In early 1994, in the fifth year after I arrived, John Haughey, SJ, moral theologian and ethicist, came to our parish in Winnetka; and after Mass, John heard my story as we shared a cup of coffee and a conversation in my kitchen. As we talked, we realized that both of us were imagining an initiative for healthcare ethics in a small community. He imagined the effort to be a freestanding institution serving the needs of those who knocked on any front door, in any neighborhood. This initiative would answer any need that the local situation called for. The "local situation" in this case was simply my neighborhood, my block, in my town. The effort we both envisioned was actually happening on Cherry Street in Winnetka.

Similarly, Reverend J. Brian Hehir of the Archdiocese of Boston, a longtime associate and friend, said: "If one seeks to influence, shape, direct, heal, elevate, and enrich a complex industrial democracy, it cannot simply be done by the integrity of individual witness. It is done by institutions that lay hands on life at critical points where life can be injured or fostered, where people are born and die, where they learn and teach, where they

29

are cured and healed, and where they can be assisted when in trouble."[9]

I had clearly been reflecting long and hard about the new dimension of caregiving in which I had been involved since 1983: healthcare ethics at the corporate level. However, my move from South Bend to Winnetka had moved me from corporate America to neighborhood America. As I continued to work with ethics committees, I answered the needs on my street. In the neighborhood, I saw unexpected gaps in the delivery system.

Neighborhoods are what humanize a city, bring it down to a manageable scale. Neighborhoods include where we live and where we work. We have common concerns; we help each other out, meet in the grocery store, go to meetings together. The neighborhood is what determines, subtly and over time, what is important. In 1995, when my home office moved from Cherry Street to the Conference Center at Divine Word International, three other Not for Profits were housed there as I began the work of setting up my ministry as a not for profit.

In November 1998, Arnold Reiman, M.D., then editor-in-chief emeritus of *The New England Journal of Medicine*, when asked what a functional health system would look like, answered: "The system I envision starts from the ground up and is going to vary from state to state and region to region in recognizing local needs. Then it will allow caregivers to work together and enlist the support of local citizens. Obviously, they will need to be supported in some way by federal legislation and funding, which is already beginning to happen in some parts of the country, but there must be no federal control of the whole system."[10]

Though I did not realize where my ministry in healthcare was going when I was on Cherry Street, in retrospect something very important was happening: The Center for Ethics and Advocacy was unfolding as the first community-based ethics education initiative in the United States. These were its roots. There were no funded community initiatives at this point, and a day in the life of this evolving small agency looked like any neighborhood would look on any one morning. Many people were seriously ill on the same block within the same time period. The soon-to-be-formed Board of Trustees and I realized that this small effort challenged the current managed care concept of "managed lives." Such a systemic concept could not recognize that individuals and families very frequently coped with life-threatening illness *as members of a community*. We called on one another when in need. We did not call on a physician, hospice, or 911. We called on one another.

In 1996, the Society of the Sacred Heart provided a grant for operational expenses, and an advisory board was formed. In 1997, we applied for tax exemption, which we received that June. A second grant was awarded by the Society of the Sacred Heart, and a third grant was awarded by the Conrad Hilton Foundation establishing an inner-city human rights committee for recently discharged mental health patients. At this time, my work with institutional ethics committees began to decrease, and local neighborhood and community work increased. Initially, I did not realize this subtle shift.

In 1998, a fourth grant was received from the Glenview State Bank of Glenview, Illinois, providing for healthcare ethics education for low income African-American women. A Welfare to Work healthcare advocacy program was established as well. Healthcare ethics education was set up in a shelter for homeless women, Wings, in Morton Grove, Illinois. This was only the beginning. Meanwhile, neighborhood work continued.

In our newly established Board of Trustees, I had people who provided invaluable assistance in growing The Center in future years. These were my Legacy Leaders. "Legacy Leaders have a private and public integrity. They possess a moral code, are committed to stewardship, have a sense of unchanging purpose, are builders. They craft a concept dedicated to community well-being. Legacy Leaders instill hope. Legacy Leaders are in truth stewards of a legacy."[11] The charter members of the board were Religious of the Sacred Heart. Four of them served in this capacity: Martha Curry, RSCJ, Margherita Cappelli, RSCJ, Judith Vollbrecht, RSCJ, and Nancy Morris, RSCJ.

---

[6] Wheatley, Margaret, "*Reclaiming Gaia, Reclaiming Life*", in *Chaos, Gaia, Eros*, Harper, San Francisco, 1994, p.126.

[7] Ammons, A.R., "Tape for the Turn of the Year," W.W. Norton and Company, Inc., 1965.

[8] Glaser, John, unpublished papers.

[9] Hehir, J. Brian, Unpublished papers.

[10] Reiman, MD, Arnold, Editor, *New England Journal of Medicine*, 339 (22) "Questions and Answers Section," November 26, 1998.

[11] Catholic Health Association of the United States, *Health Progress*, March 1999, St. Louis, Mo., 1999, p. 28.

CHAPTER FOUR

A TIMELINE

THE FOLLOWING TIMELINE HIGHLIGHTS THE ORGANIZATIONAL evolution of The Center for Ethics and Advocacy in Healthcare and shows how individuals from a variety of backgrounds and generous financial support from several sources came together in a new way to serve the needs of community members.

1989   Continuing the work of institutional ethics consulting under the same company name, Sister Peggy McDonnell, from her experience working as a nurse practitioner with an HMO, begins answering needs in her neighborhood and local community in Winnetka, Illinois. Thus, a neighborhood healthcare ministry without walls evolves. Networking with local parishes and hospitals begins. Professional and non-professional workers join this effort, both as volunteers and paid employees. First brochure is printed. The inspirational work of community organizer John McKnight (Northwestern University) becomes central to the vision. His text, *Building Communities from the Inside Out: A Path Toward Finding and Mobilizing a Community's Assets*, is recognized as being foundational to the work.

1991   Neighborhood people become involved. Loyola University students begin serving as interns.
Thomas Murray, President, Severtson Murray, Inc., and executive director of the Illinois Institute for Entrepreneurship Education, becomes an advisor.

1992   Nathaniel Marks, founder, director, Designmarks Corp., produces a brochure. *"The Everyday Challenge of Healthcare"* which acknowledges the impact of managed care on individuals, families, and institutions. With this brochure, the community dimension of the work receives expression for the first time.

1993   Sister McDonnell realizes that neighborhoods increasingly experience the impact of the cost of healthcare on their local culture. Neighborhoods become aware of a more vulnerable and sick homeless population existing on the streets.

1994   The Society of the Sacred Heart subsidizes overhead expenses of the ministry.

Board member John Haughey, SJ, sends a memo to Columbia Initiatives regarding his vision for community health under managed care, including implications for local churches. Father Haughey and Sister McDonnell realize that his vision exists in her current neighborhood. Thus, The Center for Ethics and Advocacy is born. John's memo states: "In its second incarnation, the healthcare ministry of the churches will be from a freestanding institution, where it will function as servant, associate, facilitator, *amicus curiae*, whatever the local situation calls for. It will have intellectual and pastoral competence, schooled in an interdenominational vision of healthcare in all its component parts. It will serve institution-based professionals and the wider community; it will be a catalyst for creating non-professional networks of services within smaller communities, neighborhoods, and parishes. The changing healthcare delivery system creates a great need for immediate, hands-on ministries."[12]

1995   The Society of the Sacred Heart subsidizes overhead expenses of the ministry.

In the summer, first Advisory Board is formed, and Bruce Doblin, MD, is invited to become associated with The Center.

1995   Office moves to Conference Center of Divine Word International, in Techny, Illinois, in November.

1996   First Advisory Board meeting on August 24. The Center officially receives its name: The Center for Ethics and Advocacy in Healthcare, 501 (c)(3) status received June 1998, retroactive to October 1997. First grant covering expenses for the newly established Center is received from the Society of the Sacred Heart. Subsidy covering overhead expenses continues as separate donation from the Society. Articles of Incorporation are filed with the State of Illinois. (Ratified and accepted February 13, 1997.)

1997   Second grant is received in March from the Conrad Hilton Foundation establishing an inner city Human Rights Committee, for recently discharged state mental health patients.

Tax-exempt status is granted in June.

Third grant received in September from the Society of the Sacred Heart, covering Center expenses; additional subsidy to cover overhead expenses subsequently received as second donation.

1998   Fourth grant received in January from Glenview State Bank to provide for healthcare ethics education for low-income African-American women, participating in a welfare to work program (Seniors Action Service of Evanston).

Bruce Doblin, MD, and Sister McDonnell become co-directors, February and August.

Glenview State Bank in September provides for second year of funding for Seniors Action Service of Evanston

Society of the Sacred Heart in October/November subsidizes operational expenses again. Seven requests for community-based training are received.

Two highly qualified women, involved in advocacy work and coming with salaries, offer to work under the umbrella of The Center. One is involved in advocacy work at the state and city levels; the other wishes to assist those having difficulty with their insurance providers.

Project originally funded by Hilton Foundation in December is accepted under umbrella of Mt. Sinai Hospital, continuing under the leadership of Sister McDonnell.

1999   Financial history indicates that community support is growing. Not-for-profit postal stamp received. A network of professionals offering pro bono help to individuals and families is increasing. Volunteers continue to apply.

People are seeing The Center as a place to get proper preparation in order to help with the increasing numbers of underinsured or uninsured. They see the Center as an umbrella organization within which they can do healthcare advocacy, and as a place to call and come for help.

Articles of Incorporation changed to reflect the name of the organization: The Center for Ethics and Advocacy in Healthcare; Martha Curry, RSCJ, named president of the board; charter members will be Religious of the Sacred Heart.

---

[12] Haughey, John C., SJ, Excerpt, *Letter to Columbia Initiatives.*

CHAPTER FIVE

COMMUNITY HEALTHCARE ETHICS INTERNSHIP

No matter whether at home, in a waiting room, in a restaurant, or on the street, community members told stories of difficulties with the healthcare system. Sometimes difficulties took the form of financial problems with health insurance. At other times, the tough decisions patients and their families faced were problematic in themselves. We supported local families through these conflicts by answering questions and guiding them as they navigated a very difficult healthcare system, responding *in any way we could* to family crises that arose. We connected people with local and national support organizations, all the while updating our website with links to resources, encouraging self-initiated advocacy. People did not come to us; we went to them, either in person or by phone.

Assistance was given to people as far away as Libya and Pakistan. Inquiries for the John Jones Internship in Community Healthcare Ethics came from the United States as well as Europe. Vital to the realization of The Center's mission, I initiated the student internship program in 2002 and this was due to the generosity of the Glenview State Bank. The education of young adults was central to this program. By exploring the practical and theoretical issues in the ethics of healthcare, The Center made a positive investment in the lives of the interns and advanced its mission in the community. The mission could hope for progress only if young people in the community felt a sense of moral responsibility for themselves and their community. In this way, the internship program was critical to The Center's ability to meet the community's need for help in navigating the system.

The need for this internship was also evidenced by a hunger for applied ethics education and the lack of such an education in the wider academic community. When the internship was first advertised, it was common to receive over one hundred applications for two or three internship spots. Even when it was decided not to advertise for the summer of 2009, thirteen applicants sought out the opportunity on their own.

The interns as well as other members of the community commented on the necessity of this type of hands-on education so that they could assist patients and their families to bring values to bear on decisions regarding healthcare. Importantly, this was not the same education students would obtain from a class in philosophical ethics, which focused on abstract theory, or even a class in medical ethics, which usually approached dilemmas from the perspective of a healthcare provider. Instead, the internship strived to help the interns understand the complexity of an individual's values and the importance of helping them understand and preserve a quality of life consistent with *their uniqueness and potential*. It also helped the interns recognize the potential for spiritual, personal, and social growth that exists in aged or ill individuals just as it does in young, healthy people.

The internship's implementation began with a rigorous application process that included the submission of an essay and résumé, a phone interview, and in-person interviews with The Center's director and one board member. The two to four prospective interns who best fit the qualifications were mailed an acceptance packet that helped prepare them for their summer experience.

The internship was six weeks long during June and July, four days each week, seven hours each day. It was designed to provide the interns with a more experiential and self-directed learning environment than a traditional classroom. It incorporated field trips to meet with patients and healthcare advocates, guided reading, and discussions among the interns themselves about the implementation of healthcare and its intersection with human values. They went to patients where they were, for example at the bedside, in the workplace. They gradually learned more about the values that drive patient and family decision making in healthcare. The first week of the program focused on local community healthcare, studying health problems in the community in which The Center was located. In learning this methodology, the students were able to return to their own community and use the same technique to determine the main healthcare needs in that community.

How did the health problems in their home community originate, and why have they continued? Is the healthcare problem nutritional, situational, workplace related, an infectious disease? What steps have been taken to bring the problems under control? Have they diminished, and if so, how has this happened? Of course, if the problem is a communicable disease there is usually more important research to be done, particularly in studying the social problems at the root of the communicable disease in a particular community.

More than 20 years later, at the start of 2020, the coronavirus pandemic is taking a huge toll in every community. If the internship program were being held in the summer of 2020, the research would be much more complicated, but the same methodology for contact tracing would be important for the students to learn. This way they could return to their home communities and assist in educating the population for prevention.

Each week there was a featured speaker on the theme of the week. The first week was spent entirely on orientation. There was a dress code. Though the internships were held during the summer, each student had to come dressed professionally.

The second week was about healthcare issues in the city of Chicago. The same methodology was used in order to determine prevailing health issues. We visited the Center for Health Poverty Law in order to understand the work done there. Where were the pockets of poorest health, and what were the problems? How were they being addressed? The third week focused on national healthcare, studying the main health problems in the United States and their origin. The fourth week was focused on international healthcare issues. The fifth week was devoted to students' writing an article for The Center's newsletter, and the last week was one of integrating the various strands of their learning experience and doing an evaluation of the program. The writing projects covered such issues as pain relief and pain management. One student wrote an article entitled "Wanted to Catch a Glimpse but Saw the Whole Picture." (This student became a physician.) Another wrote about an aspect of the pharmaceutical industry. Yet another wrote about "The Necessity of Ethics in Healthcare." (This student is with the State Department now.) Jason Altilio, PhD, did a documentary on The Center in 2008. A copy is in the University and Special Collections archive at Loyola University in Chicago.

CHAPTER SIX

THE INTEGRATION OF ETHICS, SPIRITUALITY AND THE ILLNESS EVENT

IN AN ARTICLE IN *CATHOLIC HEALTH WORLD* IN 1989, WE READ: "As they face the grim reality that additional funding for healthcare is just not possible, Oregon (state) and Alameda County officials think rationing healthcare for the poor may be an equitable way of divvying up a constantly shrinking pie."[13] The article goes on to say that health needs in these two places were prioritized, and the state legislature in Oregon was deciding which needs would get highest priority for which group of people. I wrote at that time: "What would it feel like if we were the ones left out of the lottery?"

When The Patient Self-Determination Act was passed, it stated that all patients, upon admission to hospitals, skilled nursing facilities, hospices, home health agencies, and HMOs, would be asked if they have a living will or a durable power of attorney for healthcare. If they did not, they would be offered the opportunity to complete one or both documents upon admission. These facilities had also to begin to offer educational programs for staff and local communities regarding these issues.

The enacting of this law was forced by technological advances and the healthcare economy. Medicine had been pushed to the point where resources were available to keep people alive for years beyond what would have been available in the past. The prohibitive cost of some technology— with no standards set to determine who got what—made the reality of rationing these resources for the poor and, subsequently, the middle class a real possibility. This forced a shift away from how we unconsciously understood the physician-patient relationship.

If we were to imagine that relationship, who would our personal physician be? Friend? Healer? Father? Mother? Fighter against disease? Co-journeyer? This image has been culturally influenced over the years. Images that physicians had of patients were also influenced by professional codes of ethics, the Hippocratic Oath, professional exposure in multiple settings, opinions of professors in medical schools, and the like. As the Patient Self-Determination Act took hold, patients were urged to assume more responsibility for their health.

In the literature during these years, the following phrases could be found: "The doctor, patient, and family will reach consensus," or "The patient will be involved in the decision," or "The decision should conform to the patient's wishes."

Again: "The patient participates in the decision," and "The patient is fully involved in the decision," "The patient is the decision maker," and "The decision is discussed with the patient." Clearly everyone was not "on the same page" with regard to the patient-physician relationship.

Moral conversion takes place within all of us all of the time, and very definitely in the sick. They are no different, except for the fact that they frequently live far more deeply than do those of us who are active. Moral conversion changes the basis of the person's decisions from satisfaction to value, from what gives pleasure to what is truly good. Though the Patient Self-Determination Act did change issues around choice in managing one's care, it was not the whole answer.

In a health center in Boston, I had been responsible for a female patient who had abdominal pain. I examined her and asked the physician with whom I worked to check her. We could not pinpoint the problem. The woman went home with no diagnosis. She returned several days later and the same thing happened. I could find nothing, nor could the physician. The woman literally beseeched me with her eyes, as she had done at the first visit. I told the physician that we *had* to keep believing in her. Therefore, we went back and tried to find the source of her pain again. I privately *begged* the doctor not to give up on her. We finally found an abscess deep in her abdominal cavity. The woman was ultimately all right. I think what struck me most was my eye contact with her. What mattered most to her was that I believed her. It mattered to her, and it certainly mattered to me.

Pierre Teilhard de Chardin wrote in *The Phenomenon of Man*: "Love alone is capable of uniting living beings in such a way as to complete and fulfill them, for it alone takes them and joins them by what is deepest in themselves."[14] However, sometimes the physical appearance of the sick makes one quick to think that this person is barely reachable. To me, though, the heart of the other is right within reach. It is "right there," and the heart of the sick person must be encountered and known. The body and its particular illness at this or that moment are only the route to the heart. I have rarely, if ever, met a patient whose heart has not been "right there" waiting to be met. My heart meets the patient's heart. In that interaction, healing occurs at some level. When heart speaks to heart, someone is known, loved, believed in, and called forth. Healing starts to happen.

---

[13] *Catholic Health World*, Volume 5, Number 8, April 15, 1989, pp. 2-3.

[14] Teilhard de Chardin, Pierre, *The Phenomenon of Man*, Harper Perennial, New York, 1955.

CHAPTER SEVEN

MORAL GROWTH: PERSONAL STATEMENT OF VISION

I BELIEVE THAT THE PERSONAL AND SOCIAL DIMENSIONS OF HUMAN dignity are inseparable. Human dignity is threatened not only by inadequate healthcare but also by lack of participation in decisions about care.

Each person's life has inestimable value. We are all responsible for creating the conditions that enable the sick and vulnerable to express their unique value. This contributes to the well-being of us all. Toward this end, my efforts have been directed toward assisting healthcare groups, community groups, and patients to understand the "how to's" of ethical decision making.

Both patients and providers of care are at the heart of this endeavor, an enterprise in advocacy, one that could well be called "Education as Transformation: Identity Change and Development," as Richard Katz states in an article in the *Harvard Educational Review*.[15]

Moral growth takes place as we relate both to ourselves and to others. The word "moral" means "right relationships" or "balanced relationships," relationships that are correct, given the place, time, and circumstances. Moral growth takes place in any number of ways, but one way is in the realization of our personal growth in autonomy or independence in ourselves. As we become more sensitive to such inner growth in ourselves, we tend to observe it in others with more ease. We do not have to say anything, just knowing the other at this level is helpful in developing a more moral relationship with them. That could be a more honest relationship, or a deeper relationship.

When I speak of moral growth, I mean character formation, human conduct, and truth. Moral growth is not something we put on every day and set aside when the day is finished. It is rather who one becomes over a lifetime, who any person is when alone, how and why one does things, and who one is in relationship.

As one grows, patterns of choice and responsibility become part of an inner ethical process and are aspects of every moment. This process I see ultimately as one of growth toward freedom, implying and necessitating openness to change. This takes place when we admit that there may be more than one way of doing things, and at times admit there can even be a different way of doing things without compromising who we are. As caregivers, our responsibility is to continue to nourish and foster our own moral growth, the growth that is, for all of us, so hard won. This is what we are also unknowingly doing for patients under our care.

In her 1994 book of poetry, *In Darkness and in Light: A Physician's Journey into Spiritual Healing,* Lesley Heafitz, M.D., herself a patient who, while suffering with terminal ovarian cancer, said to her physician: "Do not steal my dignity. Though you steer the ship for me, let me put my hand, too, upon the wheel so that I may feel I have control."[16] She also asked that neither her fear nor fear on the part of others control the interweaving of any decision process around her dying.

Being an ethical person is fundamental to moral growth. Ethics is a mindset that attends to, and listens for, the balance between good and evil in situations and events. This is vitally important because there can often be a lack of attentiveness to the subtleties occurring in human behavior. Noticing subtleties in human action takes a capacity to be silent in the midst of inner and outer noise. We are all "doing ethics" at any one point in time because we are all trying to do the right thing. In our Centerspace, or our private "place" within, we become aware of subtleties in our behavior and the slight shifts in the exquisite inner attitudes in ourselves and others.

We can become aware that a decision we make or one that is made for, by, or about others can be wrong, when the original intent was to make a correct decision. Inappropriate behavior can slip in or slip by unnoticed. Quite suddenly, observers can become aware of a change within or around them that they do not like. Any one of us can ask: Was it in me? Was it in the other?

Immoral or unethical behavior can have slipped into our actions and the actions of those around us. When subtleties are involved, it can be very hard to make distinctions between right and wrong. Distinctions separate two things, according to Professor Sharon Parks of Harvard Divinity School, but when distinguishing, we "put spirit" into the matter at hand. I learned this from Dr. Parks in her class on "Adult Moral and Spiritual Development" that I took in the fall of 1983. In silence, watching and listening with attentiveness, we become more discriminating. There is frequently only a *very slight difference* between what is said and what is done. This power of discrimination can make all the difference because, as we observe the values being lived out by another, we come to know them better and in so knowing we can frequently start to distinguish or put spirit into their value system, that is realize that there might be additional values being lived out. It is helpful as well to name what we see, both in ourselves and to the other, though this is not always possible.

As caregivers especially, we want to be ethical people. *We* want to have a *lived* value system. However, do we know what a lived value system really means in relation to the sick persons in front of us? Are we *honoring their choices*? Their choices can tell us about our value system *and* theirs. The more alert we are to our own behavior, the more frequently and habitually we can provide correctives to ourselves, the more we will be able to respond constructively when we find the behavior of others unsettling. This inner effort on our part actually helps us to help others who are navigating rough waters anytime in life, particularly at the end of life.

We need to be astute in judging the behavior of others. In criticizing others, we should leave ourselves open to the possibility that our judgments might be inaccurate. In a group setting, a thorough discussion should occur as to whose perceptions are correct in certain situations and whose might be wrong in a problem just reviewed.

In a contentious hospital situation, ethics committees frequently hold a retrospective case review so they can look at an incident reflectively; that is, the meeting occurs after a particular unsettling incident has occurred. The incident might have caused people to question the values of a patient or provider of care. People feel the need to talk about it. Therefore, a structure has been set up within hospital systems to review the case.

The expression "ethical person" refers to right conduct, good character, and an ability to work toward forming a just community. We must work together. It does not mean that a person is "perfect." To be a human being means that we all make mistakes. As caregivers, we strive to be good people, ethical people over a lifetime. We assume the same for those under our care. When we are tending to the needs of one who is sick, the responsibility is greater.

Ethics involves "attending" or listening to the proportion between the good, the not good or the less good in every situation. All of us are living the challenge to be ethical people, even the sickest and most vulnerable among us. As caregivers, being ethical has to do with choosing the alternative that offers the best or, at least the acceptable proportion between value and disvalue in relation to Self and others.

The word "ethics" is used quite frequently and people can wonder what does the word really mean? Scholars have plumbed the depths of the meaning of this word for centuries. Aristotle said: "The purpose of ethics is not to learn what goodness is but to become good." Socrates said: "Ethics has to do with the life of a community." St. Paul said: "Ethics has to do with love, and love is constitutive of community." Daniel Maguire, PhD, said: "Ethics has to do with the imagination, one's feelings, relationships, and experience." What I would suggest is that we each find *our own* definition of the word ethics, one that fits how we understand ourselves. In doing so we will come to a better understanding of our own values.

When all is said, Bioethics is a systematic reflection upon the ethical issues occurring in the biomedical sciences both in the healthcare system itself, and now in the homes of those who are sick, in neighborhood settings, and in all of the health professions. When the bioethics movement began in the late 1970s and early 1980s, moral education took place largely in hospitals and in nursing homes, at ethics committee meetings. In those years, the locus of moral education taking place in communities was only in these institutions, as the result of rapid growth in medical technology. There was no thought given at that time to healthcare in the wider community because care for extended periods was always given in hospitals.

Ethics education took place in healthcare institutional settings in order to *preserve personhood* and human dignity in illness and dying, often because high tech procedures were giving all of us the opportunity to extend life. Now, with earlier discharges from hospitals and admissions on the day of surgery, many more questions occur in neighborhoods and homes. However, there is no ethics education there. This is why I am introducing some of my own teaching tools to those living in small communities. There is so little information available for the educated reader.

As said before the field of teaching ethics having to do with "hands on" care for those in neighborhoods and homes is now called applied ethics. Some universities are offering courses or majors in applied ethics. Unless one is in an academic or healthcare setting, education in applied ethics can be hard to find. This point makes, for me, the writing of this book a huge responsibility because I know that for many, books like this one, are the way people will for the first time learn about the word ethics and "doing ethics."

I initially learned ethical theory. I then took the theory and edited some of my notes taken in class in order to apply theory to actual situations. The decision process I use helps to bring resolution to what can be heart-rending situations. This offers a method for discerning and weighing very subtle values differences that can occur when discussing decisions involving life, death, and further treatment. Later these were used at ethics meetings and were finalized as communities of healthcare personnel worked together.

The fortunate aspect about the way much of my work is done is that the discussions can take place in the comfort of a family home. There is no technology; there are no beepers, no noise from hospital machines, no loudspeaker systems. These interferences can be distracting when trying to refine very critical decisions. In a home, financial considerations can also be included in decisions made, and this information can be integrated into the decision.

We are now seeing the huge need for ethics education across all professions — across corporate America, in business, in political life, in all segments of society. There is a concerning, even disturbing, inability to make distinctions between values in conflict. There can a blurring of lines between ethics and law when it comes to practice. Law is what we must do; ethics involves what we should do.

Again, what we want is a more moral human community. This begins with oneself. With a global perspective today, responsibility for the entire world belongs to us all. What values do we want to see lived in the various communities of which we are a part? These communities are global, international, national, local, church, family and town. How do we want to live? What values do we uphold personally and why? What are our deepest hopes and desires? How far will we go to stand for a certain quality of life as a human community?

Values often become operative when one's personal values are not respected, such as when two people are arguing and they experience a difference of opinion in one another's opinion. People handle differences of opinion differently. We might begin to *argue* for the values of each one, and in so doing we come to appreciate our own value-position. However, frequently we do not stop to find out what the *differing values* are. Yet we do find out what we value when we take a stand for *our* values. Are we willing to fight for both individual and community values?

---

[15] Katz, Richard, "Education as Transformation: Identity Change and Development," *Harvard Educational Review*, Volume 51, Number 1, February 1981, pp.57-78.

[16] Heafitz, Lesley B., MD, *In Darkness and In Light*, First Person Press, Swampscott, Mass., 1994, p. 9.

CHAPTER EIGHT

JUSTICE: THE DISTRIBUTION OF SCARCE MEDICAL RESOURCES

This is the challenge: Can we be sure we are being just when we are distributing limited medical resources? Sometimes we are not aware that medical resources are scarce. Do we think to question how healthcare systems work so we can discern when there is injustice? Here we are talking about situations of injustice but also about doing justice.

At the time of this writing, I come as a nurse practitioner who, along with so many others, is living through the coronavirus pandemic. This book was not written because of the pandemic, but certain parts of it have been changed to include realities we face during this pandemic. I also come to this issue after many experiences as a nurse who, since the late 1950s, have been deeply touched by the reality that there is not enough for everyone.

In fact, that is how I came to the writing of this book: there was not enough for everyone in certain of Boston's neighborhood health centers, and that was tearing me apart as a healthcare provider. I desperately wanted to understand this scarcity better, scarcity in particular when it came to the poorest of the poor. I was in situations where priorities were set, and the people I cared for and about were not high on the priority list. They were poor, elderly, and perhaps not knowledgeable because they were from another culture or race or were not as well known as some others who were receiving "adequate care." Moreover, "adequate care"

I now realize can be understood differently from one person to another.

Repeatedly, in my own mind today, I travel virtually to an emergency room anywhere in the United States, trying to imagine physicians and nurses making immediate decisions about who gets what life-saving equipment. Obviously, the decision process that I used for so many years in my own work could never be used in today's emergency room and ICU situations of scarcity. The process I present takes at least an hour and a half to work through, and this in a conference or neighborhood setting with involved family members of a patient. During the coronavirus pandemic, decisions must be made rapidly; family members may not be present.

A word about the moral principle of justice: In Old Testament times "righteousness" was the word used for justice. Righteousness was "the standard not only for one's relationship to God, but also for one's relationship to one's neighbor, reaching right down to the most petty wrangling's."[17] Righteousness was, then, even the standard for one's relationship to the animals and to the environment. Righteousness or justice was the highest value in life, that upon which all life rested when it was properly ordered. Righteousness or justice determined the quality of faith of the community in Old Testament times. It is becoming the standard of life in our world and our times as well.

I look for justice in decision-making models that will free me to be fair with patients. How does one determine what is fair? Ethics decision models provide us with structure. Structures are meant to free, they are not meant to bind. I am considering justice not only as an element in decision-making structures, but also as an interpersonal bond. If seen as an interpersonal bond that is a constant goal toward which we strive in all our interactions, it will imperceptibly change the moral tenor, the moral character, the moral quality of our relationships in the medical community (or any community.) Ultimately, over time, it will heighten the moral character of the entire human community. Consequently, in the midst of an actual ethical dilemma, as we make efforts to correct our behavior, we will have the assurance that we are doing justice as a part of life, even if we cannot be assured that we did justice in a particular situation.

With this as background then let us examine several examples of decision-making models. John F. Kilner, whom I got to know at Harvard when he was studying for his PhD, discusses the social value of a person. Should one's social value be the basis for care? In his 1990 book, *Who Lives, Who Dies: Ethical Criteria in Patient Selection,* John lists these criteria:

1. Economic productivity;
2. Age and number of productive years left;
3. Marital status, family status and responsibility;
4. Responsibility for the welfare of others;
5. Medical prognosis and outlook for full recovery;
6. Number of children, friends, social and community relationships;
7. Society's need for his or her services;
8. Does the person have a history of antisocial behavior?
9. What is the person's potential contribution to society?
10. Contribution to the cultural stream of humanity. Does this exist in all areas of the person's human endeavor?[18]

John adds that such choices are made by the medical profession. The physician is the expert on prognosis; but once the prognosis of several candidates is made known by the medical experts, then the choice made constitutes a *social value decision.* John agrees that we must be very wary of using social value criteria as determinants of patient selection for care. He urges: "Life is not 'a good,' 'a thing.' Discerning about criteria for saving lives is not about saving "goods." Personhood and human dignity are not "things." One cannot subject these to scrutiny. John makes it clear that, in general, he does not agree with the use of social value criteria by healthcare practitioners.

I cite the example that John gives to explain how cautious practitioners have to be when expressing their lived values as they care for patients, particularly when it comes to choices for or against certain procedures. Patients are highly educated these days, but they seldom know enough about the possibilities for life saving procedures when such procedures are high tech.

For the purposes of this book, my belief is that when policies are being drafted or when hospital procedures are followed, patients are frequently not able to be a part of the process. I am talking about the vital importance of patient choice in decisions to be made. Frequently, especially during a time such as a pandemic, patients are too sick to express their personal choices. In addition, healthcare practitioners are too hurried to allow patients the time.

The list of social value determinants (above) were all pre-1990 when the Patient Self-Determination Act was finally passed. During the 1980s, it is true that patients were already entering into the decision process because culturally the time had come. The *healthcare culture* was also at this point. Decision-making these days is *not* based on the social value of people because patients now often speak for themselves. Depending on how critically ill someone is, his or her opinion or decision about treatments may be impossible to obtain. And again, adding to the complexity of the situation, families are frequently not present to be advocates.

Another way of making decisions is to use "rules of exclusion" or "rules of final selection." Rules of exclusion include hospital function, age of the patient and treatment requirements. Regarding treatment requirements, decisions in such cases are frequently based on the patient's psychiatric stability, level of intelligence, or any instability in the patient's environment. Other rules of exclusion include medical criteria, one's ability to pay, and social worth. My main point is that historically this is the way medical decision-making has been done while personal choice is of the utmost importance in our times. This, of course, puts something of a burden on healing professionals, but education is of the essence. Each one of us must know the truth. Being a healer in the healthcare marketplace today requires compassion, a depth of compassion that moves our hearts and impels us to embrace a patient literally or figuratively.

In situations such as the above a patient can be excluded from treatment if any criteria are not "adequately met." Rules of final selection include selection based on comparison and selection based on chance. These too mean that people can be prevented from receiving treatment. The final selection of patients for treatment could be done on the basis of these two things. If one follows these ways of making decisions, rules of exclusion are more generally accepted because they seem to involve what one might call "minimum standards." (For example, age and medical acceptability.) These standards are objective and more easily applied.

A third way suggested to make decisions when resources are scarce is that of *random selection*. This means that when cases are equal, recipients of care must be selected by lottery or "first come, first served."

My question in response to all of this comes from the work of my advisor at Harvard Divinity School, Arthur J. Dyck. How does one make, what he called, "neighbor-love"[19] comprehensible in a medical world where decisions are being made in such a way? Teaching patients to make their own choices is, to my mind, the ultimate way of exhibiting neighbor love under such circumstances. Patients cannot make such choices without the necessary information. The following case, which I documented, could exemplify what Professor Dyck meant by neighbor love: "P. was a 62-year-old woman who was an employee at a local bank. Three days before Christmas one year, P. was crossing the street on her way home after work and was hit by a car. She was taken to a local hospital with fractures of both legs, a blood clot on her brain, a fractured vertebra, and abdominal injuries. She was taken to the intensive care unit and everything possible was done to save her life. Four months later, she was discharged from the hospital. She had some residual memory loss, was blind in her right eye, and was, at the time of discharge, unable to walk, although it was hoped that she would be able to walk again."

Included in my reflections at the time: "I have been to the hospital on three occasions and am really going on the pretense of being a friend and simply a visitor. However, I think P. is using these visits to begin integrating this profound experience in her life. She will shortly be returned to the neighborhood where people are very much looking forward to having her back and are willing to join in the effort of helping her continue to heal." In retrospect, this is neighbor love, just slipping into a patient's world and being with them in such a way that you say to the patient "All is well, all will be well. You are wonderful as you are."

When all treatment that could or might be available to a patient cannot be offered for one reason or another, one needs to be present with the person in order to help them integrate the reality that life has or has not changed forever. This is neighbor love. In this case, P., the patient, *did live*, but with very compromised health.

As I studied, my own question became: How do love and justice intersect in a world of scarce medical resources? Will we have the courage to search for, articulate, and then stand behind the inculcation of certain values and the structures that allow for their expression? This perhaps may mean that when justice is "being distributed," those whom we have cared for and about may not be included in the calculation. Obviously, during the current coronavirus pandemic, we have no opportunity, because of emergency after emergency coming through hospital doors, to weigh values having to do with a question posed by Dr. Kilner: "Who shall live when not all can live?" Decisions about ventilators in today's emergency rooms and ICUs are made on the basis of information gathered as patients come through hospital doors. In most cases, they might be made on a first come-first served basis.

Another case comes to mind: While I was working in a neighborhood health center, a child about six months old was brought in in respiratory distress. I was covering triage on this particular day, which meant that I saw anyone coming in without a scheduled appointment. The waiting room was crowded with people in urgent need. Obviously, W. was in need of attention urgently. He was taken right back into the clinic for resuscitation. I remember being torn because I wanted to help save him; yet at the same time, I feared that he would be mentally compromised if he was saved because he had been without sufficient oxygen for so long. However, my responsibility was to cover triage, so I did not have to face this conflict personally.

I have remembered and lived with this interior conflict for years, and it is an example that helped me realize how the rapidly developing field of medical ethics could help me at such times. It took me years of study and reflection to plumb the depths of this struggle. Living with both the conflict and the resolution of this profound question has been, for me, transformative in the depths of my own being, in my own soul. The Source of Love is God. Therefore, I have prayed that the people I have cared for and about are in the hands of Love. In this kind of situation, I feel constrained by not being able to "do." However, my power to Love, now God-driven, *empowers* me. This is a matter of faith.

If we think of justice as an interpersonal bond, a goal that permeates our decision-making all the time, but especially when it comes to the distribution of medical resources, then we are talking about a process in which being just will free us to love. Love does not mean only "taking responsibility for." Love also means "giving responsibility to." In this context, Love is also education for moral responsibility. The capacity and the possibility for this involve a subtle transition (or change of heart) that takes place deep within the human person. Perhaps a provider of care under such stressful circumstances cannot *feel* what I have just described. However, here is the essence: The intent of the act, any act, performed under these extraordinarily stressful circumstances is the most important; the intent of the act is the essence of being just. I repeat: Any provider wanting to be fair but having to make such painful decisions as to not give enough to all but only to a few – this provider has performed the ultimate act of justice.

When we reach for justice in the innermost parts of our person, we are at the same time making an impact on what I would call the "moral tone of justice in the whole human community." We are contributing to the formation of a "community of conscience." In this process, justice or fairness frees us to love, while regret for not being able to give everything to everybody is slowly transformed from guilt to self-esteem and a sense of personal responsibility.

Therefore, love intertwined with justice must influence, but not constitute an ethical decision. If love constitutes an ethical decision, we run into the danger of making a decision that is too emotional in quality. When we talk about issues of scarce resources, we are talking about situations that are already emotionally laden. The emotional component of a situation can so heavily charge or alter the decision process that the outcome is rendered anything but impartial. As a result, sides can be taken in this process, and what has already been an extremely painful situation is rendered more painful by division in terms of relationships.

Therefore, in decision models that allow for conflicts to be carefully and thoughtfully resolved, I am not suggesting a purely rational process. A purely rational decision-making process can render powerless any attempt to forge relationships. In grappling with the values and principles that are in conflict, we gradually forge strong relationships. Thus, in making a medical-ethical decision, I believe a way can be found to go in the door of the patient, the family, and the representative of the medical community. A way *must be found* that will bring to the everyday ethical dilemma a reasoning process upon which we can depend, a process we can trust, and a process that will elicit the elements of human bonding. That process calls for justice freeing us to love and for fidelity to one another in situations of critical care. These situations are often fraught with pain and loss, but they demand justice in terms of allocating scarce resources when there is not enough for the whole human community.

Justice, an interpersonal bond, can assure us of structures or decision procedures that are fair. Being just means being responsible. However, what we are living through now, during the pandemic of 2019, 2020 and 2021, is not such a setting. We are living in times when decisions about the use of life-saving therapies for those in imminent danger of death often have to be made immediately and made based on rules of exclusion or final selection mentioned at the start of this chapter. This is heartbreaking for us all.

We must continue to educate for both personal and communal moral responsibility. We must learn the meaning of material, moral, and personal interdependence. We must learn, then, the meaning of deeper relationships of responsibility that exist in the human community. We must, for example, move respirators across state lines when people in one state no longer have need for as many as they did at the start of the pandemic. We must, for example, look at the map of Cook County in Illinois showing South Chicago as being overwhelmed with coronavirus cases, and then look at the rest of Cook County with, in varying degrees, many fewer cases.

Why has this happened? How can we change this blunt reality that puts low-income people at much greater risk of dying? How can not only the rest of Cook County but also the state of Illinois make a difference? Because I might be in another state during this pandemic, am I relieved of responsibility? How do we delineate moral responsibility? Doing justice will teach us. Being just will teach us. We do have the capacity to shape the future. It must be different from the past. Issues of quality of life and length of life will impinge on all of us. Learning justice or moral interdependence must go hand in hand with learning material and personal interdependence. This necessarily involves an inner change. Justice, freeing us to love, will make us compassionate. The structures will be this way only if we are indeed compassionate. Again, I ask: "How do Love and Justice intersect in a World of Scarce Medical Resources?"

A narrative from years ago in a neighborhood health center: G. was a 50-year-old man with a disorder known as Pickwickian syndrome, in which severely overweight people are unable to breathe well. He was in the end stages of this disease, with one of the more serious symptoms being increased somnolence when the concentration of his arterial blood became too low. At such times hospitalization for intravenous medication and oxygen therapy were the modes of treatment that would restore him to consciousness so that he could return home and be independent again. Then, of course, the cycle would begin all over again. When this happened to G., the only mode of transport for this patient was the local 911 ambulance. There were times when G. was not high on the priority list for transport because people knew he could "sleep on" quite safely for a period of time. G. was poor, had a long history of stabilized mental health problems, and in general was not the kind of person that one would rush to save if there were choices to be made. We could suggest that these decisions are frequently made (unconsciously) by rules of exclusion, perhaps representing social value choices. G.V.'s life also teaches this lesson: We must become conscious of the *profound underlying meanings of our actions.*

As a provider caring for G. I knew a lot about him, things one would find out only by being close to him, finding out what it really meant to be as he was. He would say quite beautifully what this was like. One afternoon G. came into the waiting room drowsy, dozing. We waited and waited for the ambulance. G. was low on the priority list. This time he never woke up again.

---

[17] Von Rad, Gerhard, *Old Testament Theology, The Theology of Israel's Prophetic Imagination,* Harper and Row, New York: 1962, Vol. 1, Pg.370.

[18] Kilner, John Frederick, *Who Lives, Who Dies? Ethical Criteria in Patient Selection,* Yale University, New Haven, Connecticut: 1990, p.230.

[19] Dyck, Arthur J., *On Human Care: An Introduction to Ethics,* Abingdon Press, Georgia: 1977, p. 92.

CHAPTER NINE

ALL ON A FRIDAY AFTERNOON

While I was in the optician's office one day to get my glasses repaired, a young-looking man "blew through the door" and walked up to the counter asking for his glasses. The receptionist handed him his order, and he put his glasses on and went over to the mirror to look at himself. He then turned around, glasses on, and said to anyone who would answer but looking at me (and I was the only one there): "I look *so old.*" So, I offered my opinion and said, "Oh, I don't think so at all. I think you look young. You have a slight limp on the left; I noticed it as you walked in, but not bad. You look great actually."

He then said, "Oh, you won't believe what happened to me!" With that he launched into the story of an accident he had been in at age 18. He was now 63, he revealed. He had been riding his motorbike too fast and collided with a car. He came to consciousness in an intensive care unit. He said he was a patient in the ICU for three months, and while there he had an amazing experience. He was "transported" (my word) to another place where people of all denominations, races, were one. There were no boundaries between people in terms of religion or anything. (He did not know I was a Catholic nun.) He used his arms to indicate expansiveness, inclusiveness.

He went on to comment: "Religious denominations are human institutions, made by us. There are no boundaries between religions." He explained a little more of his experience in the ICU and then added that he had had inserted what I believe must have been a chest tube. He lifted up his shirt to show me the scar. I deduced he had had a collapsed lung, at the very least.

Then he went on to tell me of two shoulder surgeries and one hip surgery. In short, this was a man who could hardly believe not only that he was alive, but he had also had the experience of an afterlife. As he realized the profound nature of the story with which he had just burst out, he waved his arm at me as if to say, "Ah! You will never get it!" and he ran for the door.

I screamed out and called after him: "Wait! Wait! I want to talk to you again! Don't leave, please!" He did turn and look at me, but I think he was so stunned that he had lost control with a total stranger that he was frightened away. Not only that: He knew the profundity of his words and he was so embarrassed. (I recorded this story almost two years later, never having had any further contact with him.)

I also was stunned. I turned to look at the receptionist who had witnessed it all and noticed that the optician had come out of her office during this scene, so there were two witnesses, both of whom knew of my work. The three of us were silent. The optician said, "And he had no idea of the work you do!" I said, "No, he had no idea." The receptionist added, "He comes in here every now and then." He was not a stranger to them.

In my everyday work, I do not take such encounters lightly. No one would. However, the fact that he had no idea of what I did with my life made it more astounding to me. I reflected upon this story silently within myself, both as he spoke and in the hours and days that followed. I had no outline as I composed the narrative and wrote it down for the first time almost two years later. In the way I have composed it I have tried to consider some of the following points:

Are there any roles, duties, or responsibilities being carried out in the story? If so, by whom? What are the relationships that captured me? What were my fears? In retrospect, what do I treasure? How much do I treasure the place where this encounter happened? Have I reflected upon our lives in relationship as these relationships unfolded in this story? Were there any prior commitments between those in the story? Were those commitments of any importance? What was of value in the story? What in this story says "Who is the person who was the patient"? What did we owe to the person who told this remarkable story? What could be said of his trust in those of us who were onlookers? Finally: To whom am I willing to undertake commitments in the story as represented? And, what were or are these commitments?

I have told this story to myself many, many times. I was privileged to interpret the life events of this man who was, years before, a critically ill patient. I was the one to whom the story was entrusted in such a way that I was able to listen, and I had the power to name and control the meaning of the story. This is critical, and my responsibility was to avoid abuses of this power. I have been especially discerning in telling this man's story since that day because he touched on the Holy as he told it. He knew this, and the knowledge is what made him turn and run out the door. I was immediately aware of it. Patients "tell the Holy" so frequently, and nurses and doctors are the privileged onlookers and listeners. This particular story made a huge impact on all of us.

Institutionalized restraints and cultural norms and value can become moral voices that can silence the voices of others. Thus, the feelings and thoughts of both caregivers and patients can be constrained by these institutionalized cultural norms and values. This constraint can narrow relationships, because implicit or explicit threats of exclusion are embedded in such silent communication. The beauty of this encounter really lay in the value of its taking place in the marketplace, in a storefront optometry practice.

CHAPTER TEN

POWER AND MEANING
IN ILLNESS

THE METHODOLOGY FOR RESOLUTION OF MEDICAL ETHICS ISSUES
that is presented in this book can be understood as one that
focuses on a narrative approach to decision making. Actual
published illness narratives, as we know them today, contain
many dimensions of illness experiences such as personal growth,
geographical location, systemic healthcare issues, and the like.
However, discussion involving the resolution of conflicts most
definitely should be included in any illness narrative. The reason
is that the patient carries so much responsibility for his or her
own care and that technology has advanced to the point where
patients, if able, are very much a part of any decision process.
Therefore, conflict resolution is an inevitable aspect of these
discussions.

In recent years (the 1990s and 2000s) in the United States,
there has been an increasing emphasis on narrative, or storytelling
in the field of bioethics. A principled approach to decision-making
for the physically vulnerable has been the preferred methodology.
Now, however, obtaining the story of the patient's life and
knowing how his or her story interweaves with the values of the
providers of care (physicians and nurses) and family members has
become important in ethical decision-making.

In learning the values of all involved, we try to understand
where conflicts exist. Can we learn to disagree at the level of value?
Toward this end, we gather concrete data, weigh the benefits

and burdens of a treatment, look at the values and principles involved, see the conflicts, and finally to come a decision. Again, we must first identify and describe the conflict. In doing so we can determine what values and what principles are in conflict with one another. It is extremely important that people involved in the argument know whose values and principles are whose. Then we can determine whether or not these people can see the point of any other, and whether they are able to honor a value or principle that might be of higher priority than another, and even different from their own? The goal is to determine whose values and principles should take priority, thus perhaps honoring the decision that we heretofore might not have supported for a particular patient.

Ethicists have always known that two questions with which they must constantly deal are: What is deeply obligating? What is the morally relevant material in the conversation? Stories about or told by patients themselves give us insight into how these persons have lived during illness and what their emerging priorities might be. What value priorities need to be safeguarded at this time? People who live through serious or critical illness gradually let go of non-essentials, and they start to live their truth in new ways. The process they have lived through is called discernment.

Perhaps we could call their stories "illness narratives." At times patients are able offer their own information; often advocates speak for them; sometimes they live out their illness-transformation without saying a word. The story of a patient can involve pain. Warren Reich in *Models of Pain and Suffering* defines pain as the "stimulation of some part of the body that the mind perceives as an injury or threat of injury to that portion of the body or to the Self as a whole."[20]

Suffering on the other hand, according to Reich, is "anguish which we experience not only as a pressure to change but as a threat to our composure, our integrity and the fulfillment of our intentions." Pain can be present without suffering, and suffering can be experienced without any physiologically based pain. Suffering involves transformation. Reich describes the transformation that a patient goes through. The first stage is one of mute suffering, when one is unable to speak in the face of his or her own suffering. The second stage is that of expressive suffering. During this time, the person finds a language leading out of uncomprehended suffering. This complaint may take the form of the patient's recounting his/her story. Reich asserts that patients might be telling their stories in the hope that their new Self might emerge following the transformation that they have experienced.

The third stage is that of regained autonomy. Here the person is led to the self-solidarity in which change is brought about.

How do ethical decision-making and the meaning of healing come together in healthcare culture? More importantly, how do they come together in the life of one sick person? We can be quick to think that healing has to do with emptying beds, the patient returning home and resuming normal life after being in an institutional setting. The culture of healthcare in our times has imposed, unconsciously, new meanings on traditional understandings of what it means both to be a healer and what it means to be healed.

The Physician

The function of mediation or requests for the intervention of healing was transferred to the mythic or narrative level in or during narrative incantations in medieval times. A healer in many cultures has been known as a mediator. Today's healers –physicians, nurses and other mid-level caregivers—are mediators in many respects. What is it to be a healer in today's healthcare world?

Practitioners consider themselves to be healers, but the acute care setting these days is increasingly the place for high tech surgical procedures and for crisis intervention. The patient rarely leaves the hospital "healed," according to the traditional definition. In any culture, healing refers to the union of opposites. Today's best-seller lists now include books authored by patients as well as by physicians. We could call the stories written by physicians "narratives of healers." Why is this happening?

Illness and Healing: Rituals

In medieval times, according to Richard Katz, imagery used in story telling about illness contributed to the conferring a cosmic dimension on the event. This is important because disease was then seen, not as an isolated event, but as "part of the natural order troubled by the intrusion of supernatural forces."[21] These narrative incantations bonded people with the past and created a link to the future. The "secret of success" of these narrative incantations resided in the process of mediation. This, in turn, gave a feeling of protection and security, providing the solace that favored the patient's actual bodily healing. So too in our times, the process of mediation is essential, though in the United States today we do not have narrative "incantations."

In pandemic times, given the collapse of daily routines and our usual work schedules, we must remember what matters most. As these have become our stories, there are no "narrative incantations." So far, our story telling does not include series of words said as "a magic spell or charm." We most certainly do have hymns and music that are part of our various religious traditions, but nothing akin to what used to be called a "narrative incantation."

It has been said that in Africa, in the midst of illness rituals, the "old self, fraught with problems in its surroundings, is released to a sort of ritual chaos by the divine healer so that a new Self would emerge."[22] Confession, curse and possession heretofore were seen as the result of the struggle of an individual within a cultural, structural or social order in which one had little power or did not fit. Now in parts of Africa, entire communities participate in healing ceremonies. Katz describes the transformation of the healer in African cultures. The education of the healer involves a transformation of consciousness joining a spiritual power to themselves and their community. This transformation initiates the healer's development. Healing is not reserved for just a few. The entire community participates in the ritual and expresses the need for healing. Transformation is woven into the experience of everyday life. In Africa at that time transformation was not—nor is it now—the experience of life unfolding, as it can be so frequently in the culture of the United States today.

In American culture, we have no rituals in celebration of transformation as in Africa. We have no way within our everyday culture for stories of pain and healing to be heard or told except by the telling of illness narratives or in a therapeutic environment with medical professionals. Given today's therapeutic environment in the United States, time constraints experienced by physicians and nurses prevent them from being able to listen to patients for the amount of time needed. The physician-patient relationship is seen by many to be eroding in part because of the fast-paced environment. Despite this trend, we must continue to hold fast to the constant belief in and hope that physicians and nurses hold special places in the life of any patient.

How do we understand stories of pain and healing in the United States today? Today, we do seem to have an increasing number of illness and/or mediator narratives. Because of the drive we as a people have for power, it seems that suffering, pain, and disability are difficult to accept. Part of the struggle of the patient has to do with "not fitting," because he or she is not powerful, wealthy, healthy, or strong. Moreover, a patient is frequently cast into a dependent role in terms of relating. This is known as the "sick role." Are healing narratives being authored in an attempt to ritualize struggle, to free patients and physicians from isolation, to link people before and people to come, and even more to link both healer and patient with themselves, as well as to find a link between culture and experience?

In a recent conversation with a woman who lives in Africa and is associated with a parish community there, I asked her how people who are experiencing pain managed in the culture of Africa today. I asked because as we in the United States and around the world currently deal with the opioid epidemic, finding a way to manage pain is increasingly difficult if not impossible in most places. So I asked this visitor how this experience of pain is handled in Africa. Her answer: "Relationships. They simply do not leave the person who is in pain. Very simple."

What I have observed in so many as they approach death is the "Incoming of Love." By Love, I mean a Higher Power, no matter what a person might call that Higher Power. This incredible reality becomes very clear during illness at a time of total dependence and vulnerability in the life of any patient. This is part of the profound change brought on by illness. Having seen this time and time again, I began to call it The Golden Thread. I do so because it weaves its way through the illness event, as it has through each life. This Golden Thread is God, or one's Higher Power, no matter the name by which God is called.

The orientation of my efforts with the sick over these many years has been and continues to be nondenominational regarding religious affiliation. It flows from my belief in the fact that I have seen no one die alone, or as an atheist or an agnostic — no one who has been prisoner, robber, or murderer, absolutely no one.

Though many think they are non-believers, they perhaps have done horrible things, they think they are horrible people, they have committed terrible crimes or hurt people very close to them, vulnerability at the end of life is such that all experience another reality within. The patients may not have the words to express what they understand of the presence of their Higher Power as they go forth because they are so sick. However, there are signs that the onlooker can see, signs of a Presence beyond all of us. No one suffers or dies unaccompanied. Everyone is "led forth." If a very ill or dying person resists, the body tells him or her "No." Transformation at the end of life is monumental. Struggle becomes such that a human being can no longer resist. One has to let go.

In the early 2000s, I followed a patient in last years of her life. Carolyn was 94 when she died. I was first introduced to her when she was about to turn 92. She had stockpiled her medicine in a shoebox in her closet so she could "finish things off" on her own terms. If I had told her "No," she would have done it. She had lost hope in the value of her life as she saw it, but I hadn't. Therefore, I entered into a relationship with her that got more and more honest. I told her over time what I saw, how I understood it, and what it meant to me, personally. She started to like how I saw her, and she started to walk with me.

There comes a moment of vulnerability in any life when the human heart is broken open by suffering. One can risk trusting if the right person is there. Relationships must come from a deep caring for and about another whose heart is broken. Therefore, Carolyn continued to walk with me. One night she called me. Earlier we had been talking about what kind of care she was going to need when she was discharged after one of her hospital stays, and what kind of care she would need at home. A few days later Carolyn slipped into a diabetic coma and thankfully the nursing home staff found her. Her blood sugar was 30. They gave her what she needed, and she regained consciousness. She remembered this, and she was frightened. This made me wonder about her future and whether she would ever get out of the nursing home. However, Carolyn was discharged some days later. She returned to her home and lived for several years, until she slipped off quietly one morning with a home care worker at her side.

In my apartment at the hour she left, I had just awakened and had the immediate sense that I must get up and pray. Therefore, I readied myself for the new day and sat down on the sofa to pray. I felt I was being very specifically directed. I picked up a magic marker and highlighted some words in a new book I had on the Psalms. It was directly on a table in front of me as I wondered how to start to pray.

The phone rang and I saw Carolyn's phone ID. I said: "Carolyn!" A quiet voice said, "Sister Peg, you won't be seeing Carolyn any more. She has just left us. Can you come?" I left immediately. When I arrived at her condominium, it was clear that Carolyn had departed. Absence was tangible. All was quiet. Out the window, the trees were golden yellow, at the peak of the fall season. The autumn sun was glorious. The appropriate emergency services were called. The caregiver stayed, and I left to return home briefly. I picked up the book on the Psalms. The highlighted words were a shock: Carolyn had been leaving me her last words, instructing me that she was safe in the arms of her God.

Do persons who are dying have a relationship with a Power greater than themselves? The onlooker has no idea at the onset, but once that relationship is determined we can proceed with a conversation that is qualitatively different. This is not a "methodology," though I do use one that is included in this book. It is about: Who has charge over your life? You? Another? What difference does this make, if any? I am convinced that in the midst of pain and suffering, we continue to struggle with the question of who we are and who it is that we are becoming and want to become. This is transformation. This is when God will be God. Though we fear and feel he is gone, he is right with us.

Storytelling and Illness

Technological advances, which can easily prolong illness and increase suffering, is forcing patients to come to terms with their sense of Self at profound levels. What is happening to the patient as a person? Heretofore, providers of care in dialogue with the critically and terminally ill have seen people able, in many instances, to talk about the reality of their life or death in stunning ways. Providers of care listening to people talk as they near death are repeatedly confronted with the reality that the dying are going to a place that the provider of care cannot visit. Moreover, patients often describe this as a place. Their stories draw us. We bend to listen to them, wanting to hear yet not wanting to; their stories are astonishing. We almost want to steal the story, to savor it. We want to tell others. We try to miss nothing of what they say. What people say at the very end of life does not necessarily indicate a clear change, but we often observe that people *see* something. Their eyes often focus in if they are awake and alert. Naming what they see is hard because it is of such wonder.

Before the struggle and yet at the time of this wondrous experience, patients come to terms with the fact that compliance with physician directives is their responsibility. If as a patient I am noncompliant, who then holds the bag? I do. Patients are the ones who suffer from noncompliance. In this seemingly simple inner gesture of realizing that "I am in charge of my life," the patient exercises an inner muscle. Are patient and provider able to manage the shifts and balance-imbalance of power in relationships? This should be a time of shared responsibility. We are learning. It is not easy. It involves letting go of preconceived notions that the healer is totally in charge. We work together if the patient is able to assume this responsibility at such a time in life.

In terms of resources, providers are often dealing with patients who know that there might not be sufficient resources to take them on a certain journey, yet there might be enough for the patient in the next bed or the next room. Some patients know this, some do not. It is easy to understand if the procedure is, for example, a liver transplant. Yet the fact that resources might be inadequate might not be visible all the time. Those who see and understand are presented with a challenge. Exactly what is it like to be in a hospital bed, knowing someone else will get the healthcare resources, and I may not? Maybe I do not want to continue to live. Maybe I am ready to let go. This process alone changes my very Self.

We are currently dealing with patients who are using healthcare-related community support services of all kinds, not just early on in their journey. This situation is a result of inadequate personal resources of all kinds. Sometimes people have no access to community-subsidized healthcare resources because of insufficient income. Children, perhaps, have frail elderly parents living with them; spouses are trying to care for invalids at home whether these are husbands, wives, or children. Heretofore, the whole family might have taken charge and cared for and about the patient after discharge from the hospital. Oftentimes, the patient researches the possibilities alone, prior to admission if the admission is elective.

Nowadays, patients and families are aware that community agencies are available, unlike in times past when such resources might not have even existed. People are increasingly able to be specific in naming exactly what kind of support will be needed after discharge from the acute care setting. People know that they might return home sicker today than they would have been in the healthcare world ten years ago, meaning that they will need more support in the home. Such wider community changes involve us more in our own care and in the care of others.

Patients are increasingly thinking about end-of-life issues, well before the end of life. People plan early on. They are beginning to take steps to complete a living will, choose surrogate decision-makers, think and talk about decisions for or against certain treatment modalities. They are thinking and talking about the length of time it could take them to die, how much time they have left to live, the location where it will happen, and the cost of end-of-life care. People are beginning to realize that they might just be able to tailor, or take some control of their own dying process.

Discussion about these personal issues may not be taking place around all dinner tables at night, but people are becoming less afraid of such discussions. Patients are going out on a limb to discuss issues with their personal physician. As one patient said to me, "This is the first meditation on death that I have had in a long time." (That is, a discussion on planning for her death.) People are thinking about this, and as providers of care, we are hearing more. However, one person recently said to me: "I bring this up at the dinner table and no one answers me." That is a very, very lonely moment. This is the hard reality. There is a great deal of fear surrounding end of life issues. This fear silences people.

Who can say, in a group setting: "Why incur this expense at this point in my life?" or "I am so old now, why spend that amount of money when I need it to live?" or "My health problems are such at this point in my life that I don't want to take the chance of incurring greater financial risk." How, as a community of people in the United States, will we come to accept the fact that we have to cut back on our consumption of healthcare? Who will cut back, when, and for what reason? It is one thing for a potential transplant patient to say, "I am old now, and the money that might be spent on my transplant can just as well be spent on prenatal care for a young mother or healthcare for a child who otherwise might not get it." It is another thing for someone to choose not to get treatment that is considered routine for us, when, for example, pain management is not available. What will our rationale be? Will we as a people come to the point where we can choose to get less healthcare and for what reason? Are we community-conscious? How broad and all-encompassing will our sense of community be? What does it mean to be an intelligent consumer at a time when fewer healthcare resources are available for all?

What do these issues mean for the person conscious of his/her spiritual journey? Is there a growing interior awareness of time limits or of a personal need to join other family members, or their Higher Power? There is a distinct difference between consciousness and conscience. If limits are put on the healthcare available to the aging, what about the wisdom of our elders that will be lost? Patients increasingly know what it means to them to have quality care and this at a time when their own resources might be scarce. What is happening to the patient as a person as a result of these dilemmas? Patterns for choice and responsibility are established early in life, but these change as we age and as our responsibilities change. In many areas of our country, practicing preventative healthcare is not possible because of a shortage of physicians; and the reality of chronic illness is more present. In such geographical areas, people approach their development regarding end-of-life issues much more quickly.

We make and break rules as children. Quarrels are won and lost. Peer groups change. One's understanding of responsibility changes. One's sense of self, of what it means to stand alone, is sharpened. However, the striving of the human person in the midst of transitional crises in adult life teaches us to relate to others as a self-aware Self. Crises pose a priceless opportunity to learn that one can stand alone. Sometimes, in what may appear to be compromise, one does not lose one's truth; one does not come away with a sense of failure, but of having won.

People can participate in end-of-life decisions if they have gained some measure of personal autonomy, dignity, and self-esteem earlier in life. The way one takes charge of decisions in later life will in part be determined by the way in which one met the intersections of childhood and adult life. The implications of this fact in terms of responsibility for choice in life-and-death decisions cannot be overestimated.

Through exposure to decision situations throughout life in which there is a discrepancy in thought between one's own value stance and that of others, one gains a sense of control and prepares for the weightier decisions of later life. One moves from disequilibrium to equilibrium, all the while confronting the task of maintaining a sense of personal autonomy in a pluralistic world. Under the veil of physical diminishment, moral strength is there in seed.

Patients are confronted with choices that are monumental when set side by side with issues of loss in terms of peer deaths, physical stamina, body image, occupation, and needs of family members. Families and providers are apt to perceive illness as affecting all realms of performance: physical, spiritual, moral, and emotional. However, we are living in times when patients are teaching us that in fact: "In my weakness, I am strong."

Narrative is the native language for explaining who human beings are. We are not always dealing with a healthcare problem but with personhood evolving. Therefore, we develop a narrative to explain the forces bearing upon us in a given situation. In this process, we find courses of action that will lead us and others forward. Through stories we shape experience.

Through stories we define our values, we watch others deal with the challenges of life. Through stories, we watch others deal with the skills, attitudes, and behaviors that comprise successful living. Through others, we have the chance to join groups, observe their values, and consider making their values our own. If we have not had the opportunity to be with the sick and the dying on a regular basis, it is through stories that we watch the Golden Thread weave its way through the life of any sick person. The result can, in retrospect, be the clear sign of our Higher Power weaving its way through any one of our lives, leading us to our eternal destination.

---

[20] Reich, Warren, *Models of Pain and Suffering: Foundations of an Ethic of Compassion, Acta Neurochirurgica Supplement*, Springer, New York: Volume 38:117-122, 2020.

[21] Katz, Richard J. For further insight into his thinking see "Education as Transformation: Becoming a Healer Among the !Kung and the Fijians," *Harvard Educational Review*, Special Issue: Education as Transformation: Identity, Change and Development, p.90. 1981.

[22] Janzen, John M., *American Anthropologist, Vol. 92*, p.1048, 1990.

CHAPTER ELEVEN

SETTING THE STAGE FOR DECISIONMAKING

Regarding the ethics programs that were developed through the 1980s, a key concept was participatory decision-making. Each patient is encouraged to be involved in the planning and outcome for his or her own care in conversation with providers (physicians, nurses, and specialists) and family members as appropriate. In the past, there was a paternalistic model, one in which the physician (who was usually male) was the primary decider; and the family accompanied the physician, usually with unquestioning support about decisions. Now, however, it is the patients' responsibility to find out all they can about an illness, raise questions, make plans, and involve their family in these plans as far as possible. This is a more moral position in that it engages others in dialogue about what optimal life is for persons as they cross frontiers between illness and health.

This personal responsibility for molding a quality life is the primary challenge facing the patient of today. The patient who, despite serious or critical illness, is very much a person becomes the teacher of the physician and the family in this regard. The patient becomes fully known to those who want what is best for them. The patient is the primary decision maker once all available information is obtained.

As this dialog occurs over time, patients and providers learn to live more surely and securely with pluralism in the area of values. Patients, families, and providers of care learn to differ at the level of value, to call one another to moral agency, to personal responsibility. They do this in an environment in which, at times, the line between life and death can be so narrow. This creates a personal challenge for families, patients, and providers. However, when life is *all* that is left, many nonessentials become unimportant, and, at times, one's ultimate values surface magnificently. "I am who I am." Core values, those values for which we search in life and death situations, are the most dearly cherished at the end of life.

Ethics Committees

When values conflicts surrounding patient care surface in a hospital or nursing home, ethics committees should be involved, not that all complex issues came or now come to committees. In the 1980s, only the most apparent, urgent issues did so. Neighborhood resolution of values conflicts is still largely unavailable. At the outset of the medical ethics movement, hospital staff needed guidelines to indicate, for example, when to initiate dialogue around the issue of termination of life support systems. In the midst of the coronavirus pandemic, some hospital ethics committees did and are revising their Do Not Resuscitate policies in order to clarify when life support should be withdrawn. This change is because patients are often put on ventilators to ease their breathing difficulties, but they continue to go downhill. Their medical status changes, and they deteriorate further. In circumstances such as those occurring during a pandemic, this is happening with greater frequency, often because the patient has underlying health problems and does not do well with aggressive treatment.

Changing the DNR policy does not negate or alter the way some decisions to end a life are being made in the emergency room. These are two separate decision situations, one made usually immediately after admission and the other made after the highest level of treatment has been tried with little to no success.

Other common problems with which ethics committees dealt included care of the terminally ill newborn, organ transplants, issues surrounding the determination of brain death, living wills, and healthcare proxies. In remote areas with less access to advanced technology, many questions revolved around advisability of transportation to major medical centers for the critically ill. In rural areas, decisions have to be made as to whether someone should be transported at all because if the patient is transported, aggressive care is started as a matter of course. Does a patient even want advanced technology? Differences in terrain also raise bioethical issues when it comes to advanced life support transport. Difficult decisions to transport trauma patients by helicopter, particularly from mountainous, isolated areas, cause additional moral dilemmas.

Conflicts regarding continuing or discontinuing nourishment for the chronically and terminally ill were and still are problematic. When technology has provided us with ways to prolong the lives of those who, until very recently, would have died, the question must be raised once again: Should this life be prolonged and what about the quality of life if the person lives? What about the expense to the family, the institution, and society in a world of insufficient healthcare resources? To what lengths should we go to fulfill our moral responsibility to prolong life?

Autonomy and Social Justice

Perhaps one of the issues of greatest significance is a creative tension between the principle of autonomy on the one hand and social justice on the other. In the concrete, we could cite an example of a three-year-old child brought into a local hospital. The child was near death. She became comatose within several hours and was brain dead within the first 24 hours. It was determined that she had an inoperable brain tumor. Unfortunately, the symptoms had been noticed weeks before in the home, but the seriousness of symptoms had not been recognized. In order to give the family time to adjust to this tragic event in their lives, the child was put on life support systems. The family was led to believe that there was still some hope. Meanwhile, the pastoral care staff began to work with the family in hopes that they gradually would be able to come to terms with this death, and then life support systems could be discontinued.

At the time this case came to the ethics committee, the child had been on life support systems for one week. The family still had not come to terms with the severity of the illness. The child was being kept alive at tremendous financial expense to the hospital. The question was raised at the ethics committee meeting: At what moment does survival of the institution take priority over survival of the patient? The discussion that ensued poignantly pointed out the age-old tension: "We have always been taught to take care of the patient and the family until the very end. Why do we now have to consider taking care of the institution?" The ethics committee dealt with this very real resource issue, trying to ensure that the institution's survival was not at the expense of people's lives. Acknowledging that there is a limit to how long an institution can carry the financial expense, the committee saw the need to tell the family there was no hope for the child's survival.

Ethics committees are about the business of establishing a secure forum within which values differences can be named and discussed. People learn that they can differ at the level of value and not be rejected. Thus, moral discourse at the local level has been carried on with what I would call heroic effort on the part of our clinicians. Values must be named and honored in certain complex clinical situations. This is a major challenge for us all. We are not used to naming our values and then fighting for them. This is the struggle that can lie at the heart of life and death at the end of life because, while death is inevitable, life can be prolonged.

Hospital Pastoral Care Departments

In hospitals, pastoral care departments are much older and more surely established than are the ethics committees. Today, with a great deal of patient care occurring in the home and the wider community, pastoral care departments find themselves extending their services beyond the hospital itself, interlocking with parishes and community agencies in increasingly diverse and innovative ways. Pastoral care departments are actually companions of the local faith community. Hospital pastoral departments can be and really are conduits between patients and ethics committees because they participate in extremely important bedside conversations.

Pastoral care programs assist in the strengthening of the hospital community by serving as a visible presence of the local church within the hospital. Their development is dynamic, evolving always in the context of the broader church community. Their programs deal with questions such as: Do we identify ourselves as a believing community? How? How much of an impact can we allow the wider faith community to have on the moral life of people? Does pluralism in the area of values mean disunity at the level of faith? It must be acknowledged that if a belief system exists, it does have an impact on the moral life. The "how" of this will probably be articulated differently in varying circumstances of life.

Pastoral care programs attempt to identify and articulate the lived experience of a faith community. The focus group is the entire hospital, both patients and staff, and the focus topic asks:

Is the living out Gospel values within the institution consonant with the Gospel story?

The broad context of personal and corporate morality in a healthcare facility must be that of an interdependent world. In other words, the quality of an individual life must be touched by the quality of the lives of others in the world. My question remains, then: How do Love and Justice intersect in a world of scarce medical resources?

Networking: Horizontally and Vertically

Networking in a multihospital system provides for and encourages individuality while linking and unifying at a deeper level. It appears obvious that all people are seeking a level of moral life or behavior deeper than the immediate concerns encountered in a hospital environment. There is a quest among people for a values base.

This values base could rest in the history and traditions of a number of communities. Perhaps it rests in and with the early faith communities; perhaps with the founding communities of religious congregations; perhaps with the community of moral philosophers who give verbal expression to lived morality in their times; perhaps with a combination of these.

Could it be that we as a people are returning to the traditions of these and other communities, returning to find resonance with the value systems in these lived communities? In finding this resonance, we root and secure ourselves in traditions that speak to us of strength and stability. We rediscover ourselves. We are called forth, and this at a time when we are unsure of our moral footing. We return and gather from the past and the present what we need to move into the future. Efforts made to set our sights on new horizons by returning to such value bases can contribute to the building of a renewed human community.

The work of ethics committees clearly involves a process of education and grappling with issues. Through vertical and horizontal networking among all multihospital systems, trends are identified. Depths are sounded. The more aware we are both locally and systemically of how the numerous clinical-ethical issues will affect us, the more we will be able to choose our future and not have it chosen for us.

For something to be of value, it must be chosen freely from alternatives. This process is part of discernment. Values and principles that are activated with sufficient frequency become patterns of life. A value must be cherished and publicly affirmed. There is ultimately a shaping of values to form principles.

Values represent goals or standards used for judging relations with others as well as actions performed alone. Values provide criteria for evaluation, which over time shape and reshape societies and organizations. Values are not absolute and no agreement exists as to what "correct" values are.

Principles are based on relations with people. A principle is universalizable, and is an impartial way of deciding or judging, not a concrete cultural rule. Principles provide a way of drawing upon past wisdom. If we know what in the past has been morally significant, then we will know where changes in our moral perceptions should be taking place. A principle is a guide for choosing among behaviors. Principles are more general and fundamental than are moral rules and serve as their foundation or source of justification. They are general statements giving orientation to the moral life. Most maintain that certain values and principles ought to be universal, and that these are distinct from the rules of any given culture.

Principles provide a way of drawing upon past wisdom. If we know what in the past has been morally significant, then we will know where changes in our moral perceptions should be taking place. A principle is a guide for choosing among behaviors. Principles are more general and fundamental than are moral rules and serve as their foundation or source of justification. They are general statements giving orientation to the moral life. (Examples as they pertain to medical ethics decisions follow in Chapter Thirteen).

On the other hand, rules state that certain actions ought, or ought not, to be done because they are right or wrong. They answer specific questions about what ought to be done in a given case. They are closest to decision-making. Most people maintain that there are some values and principles that ought to be universal and that these are distinct from the rules of any given culture. Principles light up the dimensions of human existence that would otherwise go unnoticed if one relied only on personal experience. The disadvantage of principles is that they can too narrowly circumscribe the moral life. In their article in the *Harvard Educational Review*, "Development as the Aim of Education," Lawrence Kohlberg and Rochelle Mayer write: Principles are "a guide for choosing among behaviors, not a prescription for behavior." As such, principles are "free from culturally defined content." They transcend and subsume "particular social laws hence (they) have universal applicability."[23]

How does each decision support the stated principles or values? The stated principles evolve, unfold, and become clear as everyone in a gathered group reacts and responds to the input of each member of the group. For our purposes here, most important is the input of a patient whose treatment plan is being discussed. What principles and values does the patient articulate? If they cannot articulate – which would be perfectly understandable – by what values and principles have they lived? What values and principles would they like to honor as they end their lives? Often patients become exquisitely clear about this as their lives near the end. Case discussions or facilitated family or ethics committee meetings in hospitals or in the home are moral and not legal in nature. What is legal is not always moral. What is moral is such because it has to do with balanced right relationships and with the resolution of conflicts in values and principles. The goal of involved parties as they discuss a difficult medical ethics decisions should be, in the end, to allow the patient to have the main voice — assuming he or she has decisional capacity.

---

[23] Kohlberg, Lawrence and Rochelle Mayer, "Development as the Aim of Education," *Harvard Educational Review*, v.44, no.4. 1992, pp.449-496.

CHAPTER TWELVE

REFLECTIVE MOMENTS

A WORD ABOUT THE PLACE OF VALUES WHEN SPONTANEOUS narratives become part of a day: The Golden Thread can be traced in decisional moments when things emerge spontaneously during any day. In the previous chapters, I have been trying to show the reader how to stand at the side of a patient whether in the home or in a hospital, helping the patient to remain autonomous when it is all too possible to become dependent. However, I do not want to imply that the Golden Thread cannot be found in the midst of unplanned story settings.

When we step back from certain situations, we may know that something important has happened, but we cannot always ascertain exactly what it is. At such times, it is important to write the story down. We should try to capture what happened in words and revise each draft until we are satisfied that it is the best representation that can be rendered. Such an example follows: While working at the Massachusetts Rehabilitation Hospital in the late 1970s, I had an experience that spoke to me of the importance of theological reflection in the clinical setting. I went in to see a patient, an elderly man who had a laryngectomy, to see if he was all right. I asked him if I could do anything for him. With the index finger of one hand, he wrote on the palm of his other hand: "22." Noticing a Bible on his bedside stand, I asked him if he wanted me to read Psalm 22. He nodded affirmatively. So I took his Bible and read him that Psalm. As I read, I noticed that he was nodding his head affirmatively, very slowly. When I finished, I did not know what to say. I asked him if there was anything else. He nodded "No." I had the distinct sense that it was time to go—or maybe it was my own awkwardness. I left and did not give the incident another thought that afternoon until my drive home. Thinking back, I felt that there was something going on during that brief encounter with which I was not quite in touch.

That evening I decided to sit and write out what I thought had happened, to try to figure out what I missed. I realized as I wrote that I thought I had done something for the man in reading to him. In fact, the man had done something for me. In his nodding, he was telling me of his experience of God. No wonder I felt awkward. It was a highly personal moment. His actions spoke louder than words.

At the colloquium on the American Way of Dying during the mid-2000s, we were discussing the importance of theological reflection in the clinical setting, acknowledging that time often does not permit this. True, time may not. However, experiences similar to the above taught me that if you can take a few minutes after work to express what happened between yourself and a patient, particularly when you felt that more had gone on than you could grasp, a brief writing of an account will tell you how close the patient really is to his or her Higher Power, however it is understood.

The hospital environment is rich with stories that the heart holds at vulnerable moments of our lives. Nurses and physicians are frequently the privileged recipients of these stories. Ultimately, we want people to be well so that they can be free. Diminishment and pain, whether our own or that of others, can be unsettling. They can make us quick to think that freedom is difficult, if not impossible to achieve. In a hospital environment, rich with the profundity of the inner ethical process, people are constantly striving for both physical freedom and inner freedom.

There are many kinds of freedoms. Death is seen by many as being set free. Restoration to health can be called freedom. One kind of freedom that I want to see patients come to is the awareness of their Higher Power, that is, the culmination of having to confront suffering in the depths of one's heart alone.

Freedom is an awareness of power after an experience of powerlessness, of loss of Self that leads to finding that Self. It involves coming to individuality, gaining the capacity to be separate and distinct. I believe that these qualities are part of the inner ethical process. They can be lost in a hospital environment. They are often hidden in medical, legal, and ethical jargon. Ethics must be empowered by the human reality. The human situation, sifted into a sentence, a definition, a code, or a diagnosis, can become powerless. The great process of human growth, that of our patients and our own, can become hidden in procedures and schedules.

Structures are intended to free, not to bind. It is easier to extract an ethical question from a human situation when there are structures for us to measure against. Structures make the break in a bond between people more easily identifiable and make the problems easier to define. However, structures can also be a way out of facing the real questions. They offer a way out of having to choose. But having the power to choose is vitally important when human freedom is at stake.

I have been in situations when there was no rule to guide us, no policy, code, theory, or law—only the reality of two lives, that of the patient and myself. As I see it, growth is challenged in such a situation not in a greater way but in a different way because no one has put out the road signs to mark the way. You are on your own holding a responsibility that no job description and no professional code of conduct will ever be able to define. These are solitary and stark moments, and our days can be filled with them.

Such incidents result in character formation, human conduct, truth, for patient and clinician. Healthcare involves all of these. We do not "put these on" every day and set them aside when the day is finished. The inner ethical process involves who one is when alone and in relationship. This inner ethical process is part of every moment. It is ultimately one of growth toward freedom, implying and necessitating openness to change, admitting that there may be more than one way of doing things, and at times even admitting that there can be a different way without compromising who we are.

Reflection within the context of hospital life can put us in touch with these realities. Moral life is there in our midst. As we uncover it, discover it, it will nourish and energize our undying efforts to create a moral community.

Obviously, there is a Golden Thread present in such interactions. However, observing, discovering, becoming aware of the Golden Thread in the life of any patient is not an everyday occurrence. We may not have the opportunity to meet such a patient for quite some time. We may not have the opportunity to watch the Golden Thread trace through a person for months at a time. The pace of hospital life is such that our moment of "seeing" must be at one with a particular moment in the life of a patient. This MOMENT is truly God, present in the constant "din" of a hospital corridor.

MAKING MEDICAL ETHICS DECISIONS

LISTENING AS I DID OVER MANY YEARS WHEN MEDICAL ETHICS FIRST came into the spotlight, I realized that I needed to write up these case studies, or *human* stories, in such a way that their very human dynamics could be elicited and personhood would be protected. I needed to be true to my experience of an incident and true to the person each patient had become. I was afraid to deviate from the then-accepted models for ethical decision-making, but the models being used were largely devoid of the human dynamics that I included in my case studies.

Being a nurse practitioner in community health, and having worked in urban locations for a long time, I simply could not deny these very personal experiences, particularly those involving relationships at times of personal or family crises. Illness and dying in the community take on meaning far different from those same realities in a hospital. Personhood and human dignity cannot be lost as one tries to resolve a complex ethical issue. I had many opportunities to reflect on my experiences in academia, reflections in light of what I was taught. Leaving academia, I then molded academic models to my own experience as a nurse who is present to and for a patient who is first a person of great dignity, now a very sick human being, but always a person.

Though each workday was extremely full, I gained perspective on my past clinical experience. I can see from my notes in these post-academic years that I had to create a decision process that was my own. I so believed in my experience. I could not deny it. I would read and reread my patient narratives carefully and would say to myself: "Amen. It is true." My decision process was redrafted multiple times, tweaked over the years, and refined. What follows is the result of my years of working, thinking, and praying. May my own experience be of assistance to others and remain true to the experiences of extraordinary patients and providers of care.

Gathering the Facts

1. What are the medical, social, psychological, spiritual facts; gather all information.
2. What are the patient's lived values, stated by the patient? By a surrogate?
3. What are the family lived values in relation to the patient?
4. Is awareness of others in society part of the values base?
5. Is family participation in a decision, past and present, adequate?
6. How able, willing, capable are family members to participate?
7. Do appropriate family members have sufficient information?
8. What are physician/nurse values in relation to the patient?
9. Who is the designated physician-leader in the case?
10. Are there legal considerations? Hospital policy considerations?
11. What are the implications for the issue of scarce resources?
12. Is a decision a closed issue? Is it reversible? Can further discernment be needed/possible?

Options

1. What are the risks and benefits of each treatment option?
2. What benefits are realistically attainable for each option?
3. What are the risks and benefits for family and caregivers?

Moral Conflict

1. What do the patient, family, caregiver want?
2. Where is the conflict of values?
3. Where is there a conflict in principle?
4. Whose values, principles will be compromised for each scenario?
5. Is there possibility for negotiation?
6. What are the limits of compromise for each one involved?
7. How does each possible decision support stated principles, values?
8. Where are the areas of commonality?
9. What should the overriding principles and values be?

FACILITATOR INSTRUCTIONS

Starting off: If one encounters an incident that seems unresolved, it should be written down or taped as soon as possible to capture the full impact of one's emotional reaction as well as important details. Once that is done, read to other people and to yourself what just happened. As you reread it, correct misinterpretations in your feeling reactions. Clarify your reactions to the dialogue in the room. Be alert, quietly aware.

Proceed to the decision process. When one sits with a group, such as a family or an ethics committee, values differences emerge as the conversation ensues. Listen as people speak.

Use flip chart pages when teaching or facilitating a group. This allows all to see each page taped to the wall. List and note with a Magic Marker each point raised. No arguing is permitted at this point, but differences of opinion should most definitely be noted. Herein lie the values conflicts. Get the information down, preferably in columns. If attending physicians and appropriate hospital personnel are not there, you might have to speculate about their thinking and resultant actions, but for the purposes of the decision(s) to be made, speculation should usually not be allowed.

As you list the medical facts, if there is no practitioner present to help, those present must suggest additions to the information on hand, in line with their knowledge of the patient.

Is awareness of others in society part of the values base? This is asked to clarify, for example, if there is a very high cost of the proposed care. Is this considered high just because it *is* high or because the family cannot afford such an expense given their circumstances? When others are incapable of carrying such an expense, who am I to expect it? I am a part of society and am, therefore, in and of this world; all are part of my decision-making. These are important perspectives when it comes to final justification of any decision.

In the past, what has family participation in the life of the patient been like? We all know that some family members are "more present than not," and in some cases some family members are "more than present;" their voices may drown out others. There may be existing conflicts within a family that put members at odds with other relatives. Some people might be "like family." Should they be a part of the conversation about a major medical decision? As people contribute their thoughts, any conflict should be first acknowledged, listed under social circumstances (in the decision process described above) and value differences considered when the final decision is made.

About question 6 in Section One on Gathering the Facts: How able, willing, capable are family to participate? Again, a column should be made for answers that surface in the discussion. For one reason or another, some people are unable to contribute. It could be due to an illness, mental health situations, or a withdrawal of a family member from this discussion due to longstanding conflicts. Visually, as each column is developed, look at its length. This step does not always make or break a dilemma, but it can contribute to the resolution of the problem.

About question 7 in the first section: Do appropriate family members have sufficient information? If one family member takes care of paying bills and assessing family finances, that person clearly should be present. If one person has a closer relationship to the patient than the others, that should be noted. Those present should be able to help identify values in conflict.

As the discussion goes on, and if the room is big enough, the completed pages of the flip chart should be posted with masking tape on the wall around the room. Obviously, the gathering should be held in a space that can accommodate this group and this kind of discussion. It is best that a facilitator lead the discussion and be totally objective, preferably a pastor, social worker, or neighbor; in short, a previously noninvolved, totally objective person.

Questions 9 and 10 are quite logical. If the patient is in a nursing home or another similar facility, then the words "hospital policy" in the model above should be replaced with the appropriate words. The presence of a patient for the discussion cannot be taken lightly, of course. The fact that this meeting takes place in a healthcare facility of any kind and not in a home makes a qualitative difference in the discussion. This is not necessarily good or bad, but it results in a tonal difference.

Question 11 is similar to question 4, but with a slight change: Should there be any alteration in decisions because of the particular location of the patient, and should that be acknowledged and added to the material listed? It occurs to me to mention here that this entire process should take no less than one and one half hours, but it is important that no one be pressed by time.

Question 12 may require additional information because some people in the group may not be familiar with the meaning of discernment. A discernment process is of the essence when making major decisions. Decisions about one's health are of tremendous importance, and there must be adequate time for deep discerning.

At this point in the conversation, everyone in the group should have had a chance to speak to the group if so wished. If so, it would be wise for the group to take a break now.

SECTION TWO: OPTIONS

Start a new page on the flip chart, and again, with a Magic Marker write down the options under consideration. Options will have become clear after going through Section One on Gathering the Facts with the group. When such a process is under way, and if several decisions need to be made, separate discussions should take place around each of them. List the decisions facing the group, and select the one decision that seems most urgent. Then list in two columns both the risks and the benefits of each option for the treatment being considered.

Finally consider the risks for the family and/or the caregiver(s). It is unlikely that there would be any risks for the caregiver, but if there are, these should be made public. Typically, part of the discussion proceeds with a certain amount of ease because Section One is inclusive of all information available, so a possible decision surfaces naturally. If it is suggested that additional available information be added to Section One, the facilitator can go back and add that; but importantly, that must be agreeable to the group so that new conflicts are not allowed to start. The time for conflicts to be expressed is only in part one. And, it is important to separate conflictual issues. Section one is where relevant information should be included, and that is over now. Careful parameters must be set at the start.

SECTION THREE: MORAL CONFLICT

Again, list on the flip chart: What do the patient, caregiver, and family want? No discussion is allowed at this point. Conclusions should be self-evident. Then, where is the conflict in values? Emerging value-preferences are usually clear, so list these. They may have already been listed in Section One. Often, as people discuss the relevancy of material to be included in Section One, a person may have felt that some data is important because it is of value to them. I have found that naming the importance of a particular value to one or another of the participants is not possible until Section Three. In any argument, when it starts, try to name the values for which each person is standing. Are they fighting for several values? No one can fight for multiple values at one time. Values must be separated so all present are clear about each. Values can then be named.

Next: Where is the conflict in principles? I have found that in conflicts such as those we encounter in healthcare, there is so much emotion involved that often people lose sight of their long-held values and dive into a fight for survival of their principles. In the context of an argument, both values and principles must be defined and identified.

CHAPTER FOURTEEN

VALUES, PRINCIPLES, MORAL RULES AND JUDGMENTS

WHAT IS A VALUE? A VALUE IS THAT QUALITY OF A THING THAT IS seen as desirable, useful, and important. The word value indicates the worth or degree of worth of someone, some thing, or some action. It is that which is desirable or worthy of esteem for its own sake; it is a quality in someone that has intrinsic worth. Faith yields values, but because in some situations values are not enough to help explain why a person or people did a certain thing in a certain way, there is a shaping of values resulting in the formation of principles. For something to be of value it must be chosen freely from alternatives. This is called discernment. A value is chosen after considering alternatives. If Faith is activated within with sufficient frequency, it becomes a pattern of life.

Certain values must be publicly affirmed. Values also represent those goals or standards used for judging relations with others as well as actions performed alone. Values provide criteria for evaluation, which over time shape and reshape societies and organizations. Values are not absolute, and no agreement exists as to what "correct" values are.

Principles light up the dimensions of human existence that would otherwise go unnoticed if one relied only on personal experience. The disadvantage of principles is that they can too narrowly circumscribe the moral life. As Lawrence Kohlberg said: Principles are "a guide for choosing among behaviors, not a prescription for behavior."[24] As such, principles are "free from culturally defined content." They transcend and subsume "particular social laws hence (they) have universal applicability."

How does each decision support stated principles or values? This is one of the final points in part three of the decision model presented above. Stated principles evolve, unfold or become clear, as each one in a group reacts and responds to the input of each member of the group. Most important is the input of a patient whose treatment plan is being discussed.

The moral principles used in medical ethics decision making are:

1. **Autonomy** urges us to foster the most freedom possible in the lives of those under our care.
2. **Beneficence** urges us to do what is best, remove evil, and do all that we can to prevent evil.
3. **Nonmaleficence** urges us to refrain from doing evil and from injuring ourselves or others.
4. **Justice** urges everyone to give others their due and to do all we can to foster right relationships.
5. **Professional integrity** urges us to know what we think and believe about controversial moral issues having an impact on our work environment or profession, and to hold these beliefs and trust in our own behavior, not only for our own sake but for the sake of the human community. Professional behavior for any field is expressed in a code of conduct. Institutions have codes of conduct. These documents (as well as job descriptions) formalize our responsibilities and relationships in the work setting.
6. **Life** urges us to respect life in all forms.
7. **Promise keeping** urges us to be true to our word.

101

8. **Truth telling** urges us to be honest in word and action and to refrain from deceit or telling half-truths.

9. **Fidelity to one another** urges us to remain faithful to public vows or oaths.

Rules answer specific questions, such as: What ought to be done in this specific case? They are closest to decision-making. Rules state that actions of a certain kind ought (or ought not) to be done because they are right or wrong. A rule can be tested by seeing whether it serves a principle or not. A judgment expresses a decision, verdict, or conclusion about a particular action. Case discussions or facilitated family or ethics committees' meetings in hospitals or in the community are moral and not legal in nature. What is moral is such because it has to do with balanced right relationships. The goal of involved parties as they discuss a difficult medical ethics decision should be, in the end, balanced right relationships, with the patient—assuming he or she has decisional capacity—always having the main voice in such a discussion.

Theories of ethics are bodies of principles or rules systematically related. They include principles and rules about what to do when there are conflicts.

---

[24] Kohlberg and Mayer, Development as the Aim of Education", *Harvard Educational Review*, pp.449-496,1992.

CHAPTER FIFTEEN

CENTERSPACE, DISCERNMENT, CONSCIENCE

I CONCLUDE WITH THIS CHAPTER ON CENTERSPACE, DISCERNMENT, and conscience because, since 1990 when the Patient Self-Determination Act was signed, patients have been given tremendous responsibility for their healthcare decisions. Earlier, the physician and/or the family or close friends were primary decision-makers for the patient if the patient was compromised in any way.

This burden of responsibility, or better said this privilege, has become weightier over the years as procedures for prolonging life have become more manageable for those with health insurance. It is in our Centerspace that such weighty decisions are made. Prior to this time, patients were in what was called a "dependent mode of relating" to physicians and nurses. Now patients have come to voice and can be quite clear about their wishes.

As we continue to move along the path of life, going through major and minor difficulties, some pivotal life experiences help us to know who we are. Who am I now? At this moment? When we do our bio for professional purposes, we are in a way writing our organizing story. Ultimately however persons have to be one with their Centerspace, which means they know who they are, discerning human beings at a particular point in life, with certain goals.

After serious illness, moments of self-understanding coming from our Centerspace result in an action, not small in nature. We decide to do something, to be a certain way, and motivation grows or not. Our passion and sense of purpose grow. Such moments might extend over a period, perhaps a few months, perhaps longer. There are not many such moments over a lifetime when we stop to acknowledge: "Oh! This makes sense! This is who I have become!" The precipitating factors frequently follow times of serious illness, or adversities of some kind perhaps having to do with employment, a geographical move, or family issues. We struggle during an illness or health crisis and emerge from a soul-searching time resolute and determined to be a certain way.

Centerspace, this place of "restless creativity where an event is privately composed, is where we make sense of an event. It is the most human of regions between an event and our reaction to it. It is a zone of mediation. Here in this place within, we give ourselves new form, we make personal sense of an issue, here we honor a Power greater and deeper than ourselves." Our self-recognition of this integration well might happen years later when the event that caused the renewal finally makes sense. Or, we perhaps get additional information about something that we have lived through, and the event takes on new meaning.

I recently learned of a family who, through a freak accident, lost their young son and home in a tragic fire. We cannot imagine what such an event would mean in the lives of a family. I prayed for them. I received a message from a close relative of theirs in response to an inquiry I made as to how the family was doing. She said the couple "are nothing short of amazing. Their faith is inspiring, and they are at peace as much as any parents could be in the wake of their sudden, profound loss. They will make it. The pain is ever-present, but so are God's grace and mercy." This is faith at work in the midst of excruciating pain. This is the recreation of the Centerspace of a couple who have experienced profound loss. The process will take a long time, but we have the sense that this is faith at work in the crucible of life as it has been in one family. Their faith has sustained them. The value system of any family or individual going through such traumatic experiences is changed forever.

Sick persons, during the worst of times, churn within, trying to figure out who they were, who they are now, who are they becoming? "Who was I?" they might say to themselves. Bonhoeffer had reached a point where he could not search within anymore. He could not "place" himself in a self-understandable way. Therefore, in a condition that perhaps could only be called a total loss of sense of Self, he shouted out! During this terrible inner pain, one usually comes to a new sense of Self, sets a new direction. Thereafter, choices are new because you are a new you.

Such periods of suffering may result in making a decision, choosing between several goods, several action plans. Just because an option is good does not mean it is good for "me." So choosing between two goods or between a good thing and a less good thing is a matter of conscience. The process involves discernment. One goal of many is to get in touch with the spirit of God bearing witness within us. If a person is a nonbeliever, this discernment happens anyway. It happens in our Centerspace.

The hallmarks of right decisions after discernment are peace, rationality, and love. I believe we are not alone in this process of finding our organizing story. If we are physically alone or if we feel isolated, it would be good if we could find a person or persons to accompany us during this time of searching. It is also of vital importance to have a community of some kind during the process. In a faith community, for example, discernment emerges from the lived experience of these people. This community can reflect back to the person who they see him or her becoming. Group participation helps us self-shape or become. Whether the community is faith-based matters not. What matters at this point is that one does not process alone.

Discernment happens in and emerges from our Centerspace. Discernment is both an art and a gift. It means to "sift apart." It is rooted in the ambiguities of life. It therefore involves a process. Discernment has an external and an internal component. The internal component is reflection. The external component is the action that results from this.

Conscience enters into discernment. There are several kinds of conscience: consequent conscience "pains" a person when they know what they are doing or have done. Antecedent conscience is the process of moral decision-making.

The moral person has glimpses of the truth. There is a tendency to make this truth the entire truth. "My perspective is the only perspective." This can lead to an undeveloped, egotistical conscience. Such a conscience can come between the moral person and the moral act. Saying, "This is the way it must be done" or "This is the will of God, the law of God" can lead to an undeveloped, taboo conscience. An egotistical conscience is introverted and self-oriented; it acts and performs according to one's own needs and desires. Guilt is rationalized away. The person is future-oriented.

The taboo conscience is introverted, authority- or law-oriented. It commands that acts be performed. Fear of consequences of nonperformance enters into a taboo conscience. This person is past-oriented and cannot function in new circumstances. Guilt depends on the weight of authority. Egotistical and taboo consciences have no capacity for judging. The person goes from knowing to acting. Normally people go from knowing to judging to acting.

A personal judgment is a summary of the insights gleaned from discernment. Moral obligation involves the assent of intellect, will, and feelings. In an adult, guilt depends on the value in question. It points to commitments and invites one to act based on those commitments. Both past and future are its concerns.

There are several levels in the adult conscience: vision, value, and responsibility. These are the conditions for moral agreement and disagreement. In addition, there are several movements of conscience in an adult: knowing, judging, and acting. Knowing has to do with a realm of agreement in the conscience, also disagreement, insight, and error. Knowing seeks to grasp by making use of sources of moral wisdom. Knowing has the capacity of evaluative knowledge, now personally appropriated and internalized.

Finally, a moral judgment is the result of grasping value in a situation, decision, or event. The object of judgment is not only the object of choice but also helps me to understand the kind of person I am becoming. A judgement or choice based on conscience reflects ones fundamental stance and shows the kind of person one is becoming. Moral failure, however, stems from inadequate knowledge or ignorance. It can come from weakness, self-deception, or from freely choosing evil.

EPILOGUE

"LEAVE THE LIGHTS ON AND THE DOOR UNLOCKED"

(Excerpt, NPR recording 4.23.20. "I Hear the Agony": Coronavirus takes toll in NY)

THE PATIENT WAS A 94-YEAR-OLD WOMAN WHO HAD BEEN chronically ill for several years. She was the last living member of her family. Her greatest desire was to finish her life fully in touch with herself, able to converse with others and express the way she felt; but she especially wished to be able to express her main values as she took leave of her friends. She did not want her thinking clouded by medicine.

By virtue of an order for morphine written by a medical worker who seems not to have known her at the level of value, she was given morphine twice daily in the week or ten days prior to her death. She had been adamantly opposed to any self-compromising medication as she faced death. Her respirations were rapid and shallow, however, and in the judgment of one person, morphine would help her breathe more easily. Why were her wishes not honored initially? We do not know, but we are left to assume that the ordering practitioner did not know her well. For some unknown reason the orders were reversed in what would be her final days, and she died being present to, praying with, and holding the hands of her beloved caregiver, this as she let go of life.

Silence in the room of a dying person is so important. The chaos that can frequently precede death is not what most people need or want. Our hi-tech medical world and those who serve so courageously and valiantly have no way of eliminating the sights and, more importantly, the sounds of machines and professionals conferring about each patient. These conversations occur in crowded corridors and in patients' rooms. The quiet whispers from the Centerspace of each patient are frequently lost in the midst of what we must call chaos.

In the long days, weeks of the environment surrounding the coronavirus, those in imminent danger of death in New York City can often be heard saying, "Leave the lights on for the EMTs in case they have to come in during the night." This chaos is a background din as people die. It is inevitable. Very few have the moments of quiet during which awareness of the incoming of Love as they die is possible. The culture of death these days is immersed in chaos. Noise, shouting, crying out, or literally crying, embracing, and letting go—this is the culture of death now. The patient mentioned in the first two paragraphs longed to be in relationship with her homecare worker and with the sounds of the world into which she was passing.

On the other hand, patients facing the problem of insufficient medical resources at the time of death confronts another situation. They may be too sick to know that they are dying because there are insufficient resources for them, but their caregivers—doctors and nurses—certainly do know. The pain, the strain on their faces is undeniable, and is silent evidence of what they know. There is not enough for everyone.

A new moment is coming for such patients. Physicians and nurses would never tell them that there is not enough for them. Conveying this or other information regarding impending death is nonverbal. However, feelings change and the feelings of caregivers caught in a situation of "not enough for everyone" or "who gets what" are submerged by haste and noise as a person is dying. Patients are acutely sensitive even when they are gravely ill and so vulnerable. Relationships in the hours preceding death are deeply important. Families may not be admitted when there is communicable disease. But relationships with providers of care can be intimate, profound, more so than at any other time in life. Hand gestures, eye contact, wordless presence, silent sitting with someone who is dying, all are perceived by that person.

These memories never leave a nurse: sitting by a woman lying on her side facing the wall away from me as she died; another time sitting by a woman and watching the veins in her neck pulse as she slowly died, watching her breathing slowly and silently decrease. Such "situations of being with" at the hour of death are the privileged moments that can be part of the environment of death in a hospital both during and outside of the time of the coronavirus pandemic. Such moments are profound, unforgettable, life changing for anyone present with the patient. These moments offer a dying person the assurance of someone being there with them on this side of the veil as they gradually sense the presence of Another on the other side of the veil.

Death is the stark absence of personhood, power, and presence. The actual hand of the patient begins to loosen; the unseen hand "on the other side" slowly grasps it. Feelings of a hand being let go on this side are absent. Presence to a person or an environment here becomes presence to Another there. *Presence to* is all there is, and **it is everything**. *The hand of the Other takes hold.* Thus, a sense of Space and Presence become pervasive. Space, heretofore perhaps empty space, then fills with Presence. Again: Emptiness here fills the "here space". Then:

"Over and again I feel thy finger and find thee."

Presence is transferred to Presence beyond us.

"And dost thou touch me afresh"? / I have been touched. I am home.[25]

---

[25] Excerpt from G.M. Hopkins, "The Wreck of the Deutschland," *Oxford Book of English Verse*, Oxford University Press, Oxford, 1999, p. 155.

APPENDIX

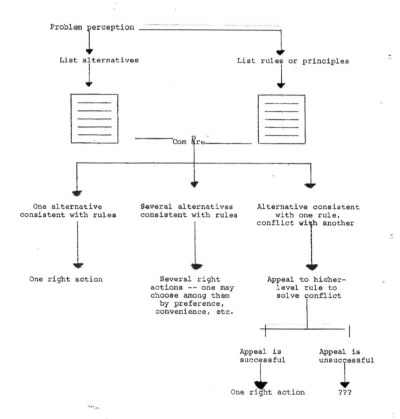

Example of Decision Making Model

Problem perception

List alternatives

List rules or principles

Compare

One alternative consistent with rules

Several alternatives consistent with rules

Alternative consistent with one rule, conflict with another

One right action

Several right actions -- one may choose among them by preference, convenience, etc.

Appeal to higher-level rule to solve conflict

Appeal is successful

Appeal is unsuccessful

One right action

???

Brody, Howard
Ethical Decisions in Medicine
Little Brown, 1981

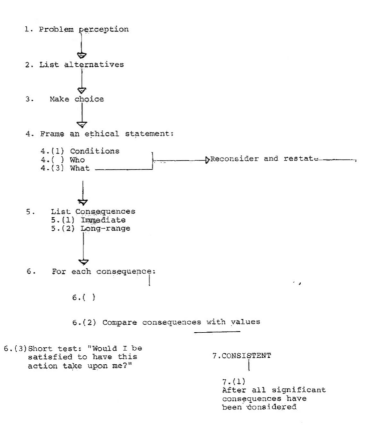

1. Problem perception

2. List alternatives

3. Make choice

4. Frame an ethical statement:

    4.(1) Conditions
    4.( ) Who   ▷Reconsider and restate
    4.(3) What

5. List Consequences
    5.(1) Immediate
    5.(2) Long-range

6. For each consequence:

    6.( )

    6.(2) Compare consequences with values

6.(3) Short test: "Would I be
    satisfied to have this   7. CONSISTENT
    action take upon me?"

                                7.(1)
                                After all significant
                                consequences have
                                been considered

                8. INCONSISTENT   7.(2) ETHICAL STATEMENT
                                      IS VALID

Brody, Howard
Ethical Decisions in Medicine
Little Brown, 1981

114

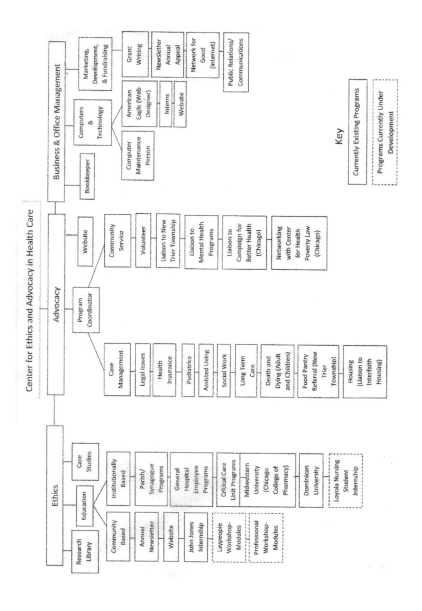

Center for Ethics and Advocacy in Health Care

Ethics
- Research Library
- Education
  - Community Based
    - Annual Newsletter
    - Website
    - John Jones Internship
    - Laypeople Workshop-Modules
    - Professional Workshop-Modules
  - Institutionally Based
    - Parish/Synagogue Programs
    - General Hospital Employee Programs
    - Critical Care Unit Programs
    - Midwestern University (Chicago College of Pharmacy)
    - Dominican University
    - Loyola Nursing Student Internship
- Case Studies

Advocacy
- Website
- Program Coordinator
  - Case Management
    - Legal Issues
    - Health Insurance
    - Pediatrics
    - Assisted Living
    - Social Work
    - Long Term Care
    - Death and Dying (Adult and Children)
    - Food Pantry Referral (New Trier Township)
    - Housing (Liaison to Interfaith Housing)
  - Community Service
    - Volunteer
    - Liaison to New Trier Township
    - Liaison to Mental Health Programs
    - Liaison to Campaign for Better Health (Chicago)
    - Networking with Center for Health Poverty Law (Chicago)

Business & Office Management
- Bookkeeper
- Computers & Technology
  - Computer Maintenance Person
  - American Eagle (Web Designer)
    - Interns
    - Website
- Marketing, Development, & Fundraising
  - Grant Writing
  - Newsletter Annual Appeal
  - Network for Good (Internet)
  - Public Relations/Communications

Key
- Currently Existing Programs
- Programs Currently Under Development

115

THE CENTER FOR ETHICS AND ADVOCACY IN HEALTH CARE

"It is through the experience of others in situations of crisis, distress, vulnerability, weakness, and woundedness that the ultimate truth and meaning of every life is revealed." (Michael Downey, A Blessed Weakness, Harper and Row, 1986)

VISION STATEMENT

The Center for Ethics and Advocacy in Health Care envisions a society that preserves and enhances personhood and human dignity in illness and dying.

MISSION STATEMENT

The Center for Ethics and Advocacy in Health Care, community initiated and community based, exists to help people make wise decisions as they move through our present healthcare institutions.

The Center effects a shift in decision-making authority so that individuals become part of their own healthcare decisions. The Center works towards changing public policy in our country's healthcare system and supports the extension of this work into the community through its programs.

Criteria Commonly Advocated for Scarce Lifesaving
Medical Resource Microallocation

Medical success: Whether or not prospective recipient
                           will benefit medically from the treatment.

Degree of medical success: How much prospective recipient will
                           benefit medically from the treatment.

Psychological stability: Stability of prospective recipient.

Environment: How supportive (financially, emotionally,
                           etc.) prospective recipient's family,
                           friends, and community are likely to be.

Constituency: Whether or not prospective recipient is a
                           member of a particular group (identified
                           by geographical location, veteran status,
                           etc.)

Progress of science: How much scientific knowledge may be
                           gained from treating prospective
                           recipient.

                           Age of prospective recipient.

Other simultaneous illness: Whether or not prospective recipient has
                           another illness (not immediately fatal)
                           which might limit the success of
                           hemodialysis.

Financial ability: Whether or not prospective recipient has
                           enough money to pay for the resources he
                           or she uses.

Social merit: How much society (including people
                           individually) will benefit if prospective
                           recipient is treated.

Willingness: Willingness of prospective recipient to
                           undergo hemodialysis.

Disproportionate resources: Whether or not prospective recipient will
                           likely require hemodialysis for a
                           particularly long time.

Unique moral duties: whether or not the physical life of at
                           least one other person--or something
                           equally important--depends upon whether or
                           not prospective recipient lives.

Random selection: whether resources are ever so scarce and
                           cases so equal that hemodialysis
                           recipients must be selected by lottery or
                           first-come-first-served.

Center for Ethics and Advocacy in Healthcare

Intake Sheet

Check appropriate box for party involved.

Patient ____   Family ____   Other ____   Date _____

Type Contact:
office ____
phone ____
home ____

Social Issues:
> Language barrier
> Cultural/cross cultural issues
> Cultural norms regarding aging/retirement interfere with management
> Inadequate income to become involved with healing process
> Family strife due to patient's illness
> Grief over new diagnosis hampers attempts to help (on part of others)
> Lack of time to investigate alternatives/etc

Body Issues:
> Fearful about being public about vulnerability
> Unable to integrate body issues with sense of self
> Trying to die, unable due to outside circumstances (people/technology)
> Patient unable to believe symptoms due to objective texts not confirming
> Behavioral response to above inconsistent with life ethic as presently understood

Human Spirit Related Issues:
> Religious issues (institutional)
> Spiritual issues (name if possible)
> Psychological (name if possible)
> Developmental issues (name)
> Motivational issues (name)
> Distress of human spirit, other (try to name)
> Personal search (name if possible)
> Ego-spirit struggle
> Trying to die, unable to personal unrest

Knowledge Base:
> Wanted to know how to access information regarding health care options
> Did not know how to access information
> Did not care about accessing information
> Inadequate medical knowledge for patient/family to get cohesive picture of problem
> MD social image impairs patient/family vision of possible outcome (e.g. MD knows best)

Public and Private Morality

1. We have a right and a responsibility to participate in civic life.

2. Major public issues have clear moral dimensions.

3. Religious values have significant public consequences.

4. Our tradition of pluralism is enhanced when religious groups contribute to the debate over policies that guide the nation

5. We need to speak out on the moral dimensions of public life.

6. We are called to be a community of conscience within larger society.

7. We test moral life by the moral wisdom that is anchored in scripture and consistent with our nation's founding ideals.

8. Our moral framework does not easily fit the categories of right or left, democrat or republican. **How does every platform touch personhood, human life, and human dignity?** (See Martin Marty)

9. Responsible citizenship is a virtue.

10. Participation in the political process is a moral obligation

10A. Being a participant in the political process means that the person is:

> Informed…..Active…..Responsible

11. The new millennium requires a new kind of politics, focused more on moral principles than on the latest polls.

12. New millennium asks us to focus more on narratives that nourish the imagination not on narratives that drag us down. (good stories)

13. There is a need to focus on the pursuit of the common good than on the demands of special interest groups.

14. What IS faithful citizenship?

> Consistently participating in public life?

> Bringing moral convictions to public life?

> View these responsibilities through the eyes of faith.

15. Challenges that surround us:

Lack of respect for life in numerous ways

Poverty

Violence

C:\Documents and Settings\Peggy\My Documents\Leadership\Public_and_Private_Morality.doc

MORAL ENVIRONMENT

Environment - (Websters) "All of the conditions surrounding and effecting the development of an organism or a group of organisms."

Environment - (for the purpose of this discussion) includes any defined group, whether it be a team, a small group, a department, reporting relationship. It includes systemic and institutional cultures, the "culture" within a given unit, etc.

Moral Environment - Ethics has to do with relationships. Community building is the ultimate result. When relationships are awry, an ethical conflict often exists. People see things differently for valid reasons. A moral environment is one in which people work at setting relationships right. It is an environment in which people are willing to bring their differences, which in all likelihood are values differences, to a "table". (i.e. a conversation, whether the table is there or not!) People are willing to talk and disagree at the level of value. The conversation needs to be structured. Value priorities for a given situation can be determined in this setting. A moral environment is always a goal.

Value Priorities - Institutions, Professions and Individuals have their own moral codes. In a values conflict we must sort out whether or not the conflict is in one or several of these categories. (I find it is usually a conflict over personal values.)

Ethical Behavior - In this setting, perhaps: What is compassionate behavior? Healing behavior? What do compassionate behavior or healing behavior look like? Compassion or healing, if one or both are agreed upon values, would be manifested in behaviors and attitudes.

Moral *Development* - Refers to the unfolding, over time, of ethical behavior by a constant willingness to look at both "light" and "dark" sides of behavior, and how these behaviors impact the group. (see attached)

Historically, moral development had been viewed in a "stage approach process". A person or a group reaches a certain stage of development (This stage development may be associated with chronological age, but not necessarily so. e.g. martyrs, heroes/heroines). This involves both cognitive and emotional aspects of growth. In stage approach theory moral principles guide growth. (e.g. what must I do to be a just person?)

Moral development can also be referred to as human development. That is, our growth might be in stages, but we might move from situation to situation, and grow as humans through dealing with conflictual life situations. Conflict is creative of moral growth. So, another approach to evaluating moral development - human development, is through the "case method". Not that we never use moral principles. We do, but balancing these with the life situation.

In order to flesh out the "how-to's" for the study of the impact of a moral environment on patient, staff, community, and the state of the art practice of psychiatry Madden it is important to begin not with theory, but with practice.

12/93
C:\WPWIN60\WPDOCS\EDUCTOLS.4\MRLENVIR.93
MICROSOFT WORD: MORAL ENVIRONMENT

In 2010, Gabriel Zeis, OFM, then President of St. Francis University, visited The Center for Ethics and Advocacy in Healthcare at Techny, Illinois. Seeing the efforts of the Religious of the Sacred Heart, the people of New Trier Township and the Society of the Divine Word in their providing space for this organization and the student interns, awarded Sister Peggy McDonnell, RSCJ, an honorary doctorate in recognition of the contribution this initiative had made to the health and well-being of the local community.

The text of the honorary doctorate reads:

"Wherever people cherish freedom and human dignity, they recognize the power and knowledge to contribute to the freedom, the dignity, and the welfare of all. It is appropriate, therefore, that St. Francis University honors those who have distinguished themselves by uncommon achievements and have used their knowledge and their personal resources for the benefit of all. As an academic community, we are privileged to render tribute to the example of those whom we honor, and we can only enrich ourselves by emulating the qualities that they so admirably personify. Accordingly, we confer upon Mary Margaret McDonnell, RSCJ the title and degree of Doctor of Humane Letters, which grant to the honoree all the rights, privileges and insignia traditionally bestowed on those receiving this degree. So that all may know of this honor, St. Francis University presents this document, confirmed with the signature of the president and with the seal of the University."

May 9, 2010.

BIBLIOGRAPHY

Aamons, A.R., "Tape for the Turn of the Year", W.W. Norton and Company, Inc., W.W. Norton, 1965.

Abraham, Ralph. *Chaos, Gaia, Eros: A Chaos Pioneer Uncovers the Three Great Streams of History.* San Francisco: Harper, 1994.126.

Aschenbrunner, George, SJ. Unpublished Paper.

Catholic Health Association, Catholic Health World, Volume 5, Number 8, April 15, 1989.

de Chardin, Pierre Teilhard, The Making of a Mind: Letters from a Soldier Priest, 1914-1919, Harper and Row, 1965.

de Chardin, Pierre Teilhard, The Phenomenon of Man. Harper Perennial. 1955.

Dyck, Arthur J., On Human Care: An Introduction to Ethics, Abingdon Press, 1977.

Glaser, John W. and Ronald P. Hamel, eds. Published in Three Realms of Managed Care, Center for Healthcare Ethics, Orange, CA, Pg.ix.

Guttman, Amy and Jonathon D. Moreno. Everybody Wants to Go To Heaven But Nobody Wants to Die. Liveright Publishing Corporation, New York. 2019.

Haughey, John, SJ. Excerpt, Letter to Columbia Initiatives.

Heafitz, Lesley B., In Darkness and in Light, First Person Press, 25 Allen Rd., Swampscott, Massachusetts, 01907.

Hehir, J. Brian, Unpublished Paper.

Janzen, John. <u>American Anthropologist</u>. Review of Anita Jakobson-Widding's collection of Culture, Experience and Pluralism: Essays on African Ideas of Illness and Healing. Vol. 92, 1990.

Ricks, Christopher ed. <u>Oxford Book of English Verse</u>, Oxford University Press, 1999.

Katz, Richard. "Education as Transformation: Identity Change and Development", <u>Harvard Educational Review</u>, Volume 51, (1), February 1981.

Katz, Richard. "Education among the !Kung and the Fijians", <u>Harvard Educational Review</u>. Volume 51, pp. 57-78

Kilner, John Frederick, <u>Who Lives, Who Dies? Ethical Criteria in Patient Selection</u>, New Haven, Connecticut, Yale University Press, 1990.

Kohlberg, Lawrence and Rochelle Mayer, "Development as the Aim of Education", <u>Harvard Educational Review</u>, Vol. 42, No.4, Nov. 1972.

Reich, Warren Thomas, "Models of Pain and Suffering: Foundations of an Ethic of Compassion". <u>Acta Neurochirugica Supplementum</u>, Springer-Verlag Publishers. Volume 38, 1987.

Reiman, Arnold, MD. Ed., <u>New England Journal of Medicine</u>. Questions and Answers Section, November 29, 1998.

Rilke, Maria, <u>Letters to a Young Poet, Selected Poems</u>, Methuen, NJ. 1986.

Patient Self Determination Act of 1990, (H.R.4449):https:///www.congress.gov./bill.101st Congress/ House Bill/4445

Von Rad, Gerhard. <u>Old Testament Theology: Theology of Israel's Prophetic Traditions</u>. Harper and Row. Vol. 1, 1962. Pg.370.

Wheatley, Margaret. "Reclaiming Gaia, Reclaiming Life", <u>Chaos, Gaia, Eros</u>, Harper-San Francisco, 1994.

Printed in the United States
by Baker & Taylor Publisher Services